Mary Eleanor ~

a child's memoir

Amey J Jones†

Foreword and editing by

Lesley Jones

Mary Eleanor ~

a child's memoir

**CUCKOO'S
NEST
PRESS**

First edition
ISBN: 978-1-7395979-0-0
ISBN: 978-1-7395979-1-7
Cover art by Eclipse Studios

'And the thoughts of
youth are long, long
thoughts.'

HENRY WADSWORTH LONGFELLOW

Foreword
by Lesley Jones

The story that follows was written by Amey Jane Jones (née Lewis) in 1930, when she lived at a house called Estyn Grange in Hope, near Wrexham. It is the account of her arrival in Wales as a ten-year-old child, and in the story she refers to herself as Mary Eleanor ('ME'). Amey's husband was Thomas Jones, a famous and decorated sea captain whose adventures and voyages were documented by Amey until his retirement. But this book is about Amey, although it was dedicated to 'the boy in the pew in front' – Thomas.

Amey was my great-grandmother. She was born on 23 August 1872 in Upton-Cum-Chalvey, near Slough, Buckinghamshire. Her father was John Lewis, whose family had lived in the area for generations and whose ancestors can be traced back to the sixteenth century. Amey's mother was Elizabeth Jones, who was born in Tre'ddol, Ceredigion, but who left home and made the then very long journey to London (presumably to find work) some time between 1861 and 1865. John and Elizabeth were married in 1865, and Amey was their fourth child.

What went through their minds in the eight years after their marriage? For many people, just having five children would be enough. In that time, however, they came to the decision that they should leave England for America and a new start. There was certainly a trend of emigration during this period. They headed for New Hampshire with their five children, one of whom was a newborn baby, where they arrived in 1874. John became naturalised in 1877, and the couple had another three children. Elizabeth died in January 1882 aged only thirty-nine. So John, with eight children in a relatively new country, did what might be expected and remarried, and the first of two more children was born in July 1883.

Despite extensive research, we cannot determine what prompted the family to make what must have been a very difficult decision to send ten-year-old Amey to Wales (where she had never been, having emigrated to the US at the age of two) to live with her Aunt Susannah, Elizabeth's older sister. There aren't any anecdotal family stories as to the reason, either, except a vague memory of my own of being told that Amey 'didn't get on with' her new stepmother. This is difficult to accept though, having read the account that follows. In Chapter 2, we read 'The dolly so loved by her had been the gift of those who were far away across that big sea that held her fascinated … and the length of the distance separating her from the very ones who had sewn the doll's clothes, and knitted her bonnet, and made them all to "put on and off" so that [Amey] could dress and undress her treasure whenever she pleased.' Clearly, her family had cared deeply enough for Amey to carefully put together what must have been a sort of child's trousseau.

Later in the book, Amey describes Aunt Han's (and also gives her full name – Hannah Berry) blueberry biscuits which were 'light as air'. Hannah Berry was Amey's stepmother's older sister. It's clear from the 1880 US census that the Lewises and the Berrys lived fairly close to each other (their records are both on sheet 284 of the census for Milton, Strafford, New Hampshire), and it's possible that Hannah became a courtesy aunt some time before Olive Berry became Amey's stepmother.

In *Mary Eleanor*, Amey refers to herself as being ten years old, a birthday she would have celebrated on 23 August 1882, which would mean she would have arrived in Wales after this. In the first chapter of *Mary Eleanor*, she says she has arrived 'recently' at the seaside village where she lived with her aunt. She then mentions 'early spring cleaning', so perhaps the first chapter refers to the spring of 1883. The village referred to is Borth, although it isn't named in the story, but we know this was where Amey lived with Aunt Susannah – we even know in which house.

She was admitted to Borth National School in October 1882 according to the records held in the Welsh National Archives. Her name is spelled Amy (a common mistake), but for some reason her birth date is given as 5 June 1872. All other records give her birth date as 23 August 1872. The US census for 1880 was taken with information as of 1 June 1880, and in that her age is given as 7, which would be correct for either birth date. Surprisingly, in the school record, her parents are stated to be John and Jane, not Elizabeth or even Olive – unless Susannah referred to her sister as Jane (their mother's name) because it was simpler. Stranger things have happened!

Amey's date of birth is given (presumably by she herself as an adult) on a passenger list from Hamburg to the UK as 23 August 1872, so I presume this must be the correct date and the school got it wrong. She also appears in the England & Wales civil registration birth index for July-August-September 1872, so it looks as if our August date is correct.

So when did Amey arrive from the US? It seems that there are few, if any, lists of passengers arriving in the UK from the US pre-1890, so we have no way of knowing the actual date. As I've mentioned, *Mary Eleanor* tells us she was ten, and Amey's 'Reverie – My Rings' (another piece of her writing in my possession) confirms this, so we assume some time in 1882. There exists an entry for a John Lewis of more or less the right age, by himself, returning to the USA on 26 June 1882, so he may have been returning after taking Amey to Borth (and was the school's birth date of 5 June given to coincide with the date of her arrival?), but this John is listed as a miller. Our John was a bookkeeper. Having said that, if we assume a trip of around ten days in either direction, and a stay in the UK of perhaps two weeks, he would have had to leave his home at the end of May 1882, just five months after Elizabeth's death. There's an entry for another John Lewis aged eighteen entering on 4 September 1882; is eighteen perhaps a little young for John Winchcombe Lewis to be escorting his little sister across the Atlantic? It's not impossible. John senior would need to have been at home in New Hampshire in or around October 1882, assuming his first child with Olive was full term.

All we can be certain of is that she did arrive, around the age of ten, and that she remained on cordial terms with her father and siblings. There are records of several visits by Amey to America, John Lewis visited Amey on at least two occasions, and in 'My Rings', Amey describes a very special little ring given to her by her father before she left for Wales.

In 1930, by which time she was a grandmother, Amey decided to write an account of her first year in Borth. That account is now over ninety years old and describes life in a small Welsh village 140 years ago. For a historian, this can only be gold dust. For a descendant, it's priceless. Amey arrived in the little seaside village speaking only English, which was then a second language to only a few of the residents. To have made the strides she did, and so quickly, is testament to her intelligence and perseverance.

I don't want to spoil your discovery of the treasures contained in the story. Amey describes some everyday tasks and routines that are now lost to us. The image of the striped petticoats of the women as they cleaned their steps is wonderful, and we can sympathise with Amey's need to swallow her smile as she watched the old man who was moved to tears in church. We learn about Amey's walk to collect butter from a farm, about school and church, about the herring season and how the large catch was preserved to feed the villagers over winter. Could we imagine today that instead of popping out for a bag of potatoes, our supply would come from two rows in a field shared with other villagers? In the last chapter, Amey tells us about the regular hiring fairs that potential employers would attend in the hope of finding servants.

Amey uses language that we would not use today (chapter five), but I have only lightly edited the text so you can appreciate it in context.

Several years after the events of *Mary Eleanor*, Amey wrote what she referred to as a 'Secret Diary', which sadly she didn't keep for very long, but in which she recorded her special relationship with Thomas Jones (whose name is blanked out in the writing as was common in those days), talking about the thrill of seeing him in chapel, or of standing next to him at the piano, and her fears about what would happen when he went to sea. I debated about including some pieces from the diary in this book, but decided I would respect her privacy and keep the diary secret. Thomas earned his Captain's Certificate in 1894, and he and Amey were married in 1896. Over the course of their marriage, they moved home many times, usually when Thomas was away at sea. Amey liked to surprise him!

I have several other pieces of Amey's writing, in English and Welsh, showing both her romantic and her practical sides.

As a professional editor, I tried to imagine how my own great-grandmother would take to me examining her text with a view to publication, and I came to the conclusion that she would be pleased. There is evidence in the original typewritten manuscript of corrections and self-editing. All I have done to prepare this manuscript is to correct some punctuation errors and fix some typos, and reorder a couple of dialogue tags. I want Amey to be read as she herself wrote.

I hope you, the reader, will enjoy the story of 'ME' – the first year of an American girl in Wales.

Lesley Jones
Chester
August 2022

MARY ELEANOR

by

A. J. J.

Dedicated

to

the Boy in the Pew in Front

CHAPTER 1

MARY ELEANOR'S NEW HOME
AND COUNTRY

Mary Eleanor was ten years old. As she stood leaning back against the old sea groynes, watching the setting sun sink to rest in a bank of clouds that seemed to merge into the waters of the ocean, her face gradually lost its usual animated expression and reflected the serious contemplative mood which more frequently obsessed her of late.

That the 'thoughts of youth are long, long thoughts' was a truism in the case of Mary Eleanor, and the events of her young life in the preceding eighteen months or so had caused her to develop a habit of self-communion that was destined to form her character on unusual lines, and made the child of tender years thoughtful and wise beyond her age.

The sun, sinking lower into the bank of cloud, was ever changing the shades of colour around, and Mary Eleanor, who instinctively responded to the beauty of Nature in any form, kept wondering eyes on the constantly varying glories of the sunset.

From brightest shades of red tinged with gold deepening into marvellously intense rich tones of purple that wonderful cloud bank changed, as the sun appeared to settle into a downy resting place of clouds for the night, itself being transformed into a red ball of fire as it dropped into the horizon with Mary Eleanor's eyes fixed thoughtfully and longingly on the fast-vanishing orb.

She often watched the sunset clouds and loved to see them heap themselves together like great piles of warm woolly blankets, and as the sun dropped into the west, she always sent with it a silent 'Goodnight' to those whom she knew would see it beyond that broad expanse of ocean which now separated them from her.

Resting apparently on the very edge of the distant ocean for an instant, prior to dropping from sight, suddenly to Mary Eleanor's astonished vision a tiny piece seemed to be nicked out of the northern side of the red ball. Slowly and yet surely it advanced across the face of the sun, and gradually took the form of a little sailing vessel coming into full view against the golden-red background ere one third of the sun had disappeared.

Breathless, lest she lose one instant of the rare picture, she watched the little vessel cross into the darkness of the other side.

'Oh!' she exclaimed. 'That was worth waiting for, even if I am feeling hungry enough to eat anything! I shall always remember the little ship on the sea in the setting sun. I wonder if anyone else saw it.'

With a goodbye wave to the magnificent western skyscape, she hurriedly clambered up the old sea fence to the house, her face brightened by the pretty little incident which had diverted her mind from a too-long dwelling on matters over-serious for her tender years.

When asked what made her look so pleased, she told her aunt, between satisfying bites of bread and butter, of the way the little ship on the horizon had crossed the face of the setting sun and what a pretty picture it made.

She wondered whether when she grew up she would be able to draw or paint little pictures like that if she could remember them all until she had learned how to be an artist.

She was told that her present duty was to attend diligently to her school lessons and not get into the habit of dreaming of impossible things, for unless people were very rich, it was not possible to pay for being taught such fine things as drawing and painting.

Mary Eleanor longed intensely to be something worthwhile when she grew up. Just what that something worthwhile would be, she had not yet determined; there were so many things in which she would like to excel. It may be that an inward urge to gratify her love of the beauty of sound and sight made her grasp and appreciate every little incident in which she could detect these qualities. In the present time of her life, she was handicapped in her endeavour by the intensely practical views of those among whom her lot was cast, and she had begun to realise that mention of aspirations beyond the ordinary was always met with advice to attend to existing duties and not dwell on the unattainable.

The continual reiteration of this well-meant advice did not, however, discourage her. While it had the effect of making her less communicative, it also established in her a habit of self-communing, which tended to make her a quiet reserved child.

Her active and alert mind absorbed much

through observation, and Nature, ever sympathetic, helped to solve her problems by presenting great diversity of moods in that little seaside village, moods which Mary Eleanor learned to appreciate with increasing interest as the seasons passed by.

She consoled herself with the thought that the future would solve the problem of what she would do when she grew up. So many unexpected things had happened to her of late that she came to the conclusion that circumstances unfolded themselves romantically enough for her just at present.

She had recently been through the unusual, at that time, experience of coming across the Atlantic to relatives in Wales, and had met with a great many things in her new country that were new in custom and manner.

The language of the village was almost entirely Welsh then, and the schoolchildren spoke Welsh for the greater part of their conversation. Few of the children spoke English fluently, and many carried on a conversation by introducing Welsh names and phrases, the mixture sounding queer to Mary Eleanor, who had not heard a word of Welsh prior to her advent to the little village on the shores of Cardigan Bay.

On attending Sunday School, she used an English–Welsh Testament, and this helped her a great deal in learning the meaning of some of the words. She committed to memory, as did her classmates, many a chapter and psalm in Welsh, but in the privacy of her room, she often smiled at the funny sounds as she said them over, parrot-like, and when she was given a Welsh hymn book as a reward for reciting in Welsh in the evening service a long chapter from Isaiah, she felt justified in being proud of having attained some degree of proficiency in the pronunciation of the difficult language, even if she did not understand the big words.

It was by parrot-like repetition alone that she could commit to memory the sounds of the words, and there was nothing to assist her beyond the seemingly meaningless jargon of sound, if memory failed her in any sentence, to pick up the thread of whatever she recited. It was best to start over again.

She dutifully went with the rest of those of her age on Sunday nights down to the rostrum after the preaching service was over, to recite a verse of the Bible. For the first few weeks she used English but was taught Welsh verses as soon as she could repeat them.

At first she found her tongue grew thick and awkward and fond of confusing the sequence of the sounds, the verses she learned and could repeat at home glibly and with assurance proving difficult to enunciate when recited during the trying ordeal experienced each Sabbath evening.

In particular she dreaded the Sunday evenings when ministers unacquainted with her occupied the pulpit and heard the children recite their verses. Because she had accomplished the recitation in Welsh of a verse, it did not follow that she understood it, and when the minister chose to ask a question pertaining to it, she could only look up wonderingly at him, until someone in the neighbourhood helped out with a whisper that seemed to Mary Eleanor's sensitive soul to reverberate throughout the chapel, and draw everyone's attention to her, 'Saesnes yw hi.' (She is English.)

It seemed to her that each day brought new problems to solve. She had been astounded when change was first given her for a silver sixpence – six enormous pieces of money appeared those first pennies she had seen. They were so very much bigger than the cents she had been used to in America that she at first thought that a mistake had been made.

The trains were so different, too. In this new country they called the locomotives 'engines', and the engines had whistles to attract attention and not bells, and no one knew what a cow-catcher was!

Mealtimes were different. It was some time before she could get used to the early afternoon tea, a meal unknown to her before. Six o'clock supper had always been the next meal following the noon repast. However, as her hunger was apparently never satisfied for long, she reasoned it was a fortunate change for her – she was ever so hungry after school and play and the extra meal was much relished.

The houses of the village were all built of stone or brick, while she had come from a village where all the homes, whether tiny cottages or big residences, were built of wood.

On Saturday mornings she liked to watch the women of the village go through the daily ritual of cleaning the front doorsteps. She saw them bring out buckets and cloth and brushes to scrub the slate slab that formed the approach to the front doors. They picked up their dress skirts and folded them up to the waist, exposing to view the striped petticoat of Welsh flannel, generally the product of a flannel mill in a nearby village, and worn by the majority of the women; then, by a deft turn, the dress skirt was twisted over at the back in a manner that safely kept it up during the time necessary to perform the wet task of scrubbing the stone steps, which they took care were not trodden on before they got dry lest they look carelessly washed.

The patterns of these Welsh petticoats varied in colour and width and stripe, but were invariably vertically striped and plainly sewn together without gore or cut, lasting for years by dint of being turned top to bottom when frayed, or even occasionally made with a tuck to let down, if the material was not too coarse and heavy.

When duties such as washing the floor or stone steps were undertaken, an apron of coarse sacking (ffedog frâs) was worn to protect these petticoats, and the women's appearance in consequence appeared comical to Mary Eleanor.

So many things that were new and different to Mary Eleanor's former life were met with that she ceased to remark about them as she found that since they were habitual to the people to the people of the village there was nothing extraordinary about them; she dropped into the habit of taking note mentally, lest she gave offence by inadvertence.

The sea, a new feature in her life, was a great attraction. Her little bedroom window looked out over the sea and she watched it daily on rising, unceasingly fascinated by the picture.

Great white billowy waves rolling shoreward, and then sliding gently, bubbled with white froth, back to the ocean, only to be met by other overwhelming billows of greater insistence that sent froth and bubbles still higher up over the almost level sandy beach, themselves meeting with an onslaught from succeeding waves, each with a greater urge to reach beyond the preceding wave's highest flow.

And then, when the tide had become full, to watch for the seven or eight big rollers that broke, as her aunt called it, 'bla'n trai', just at the turn of the conflict between the forces of ebb and flow.

Or, with a strong easterly wind blowing offshore, to note the waters quietly forcing their way with irresistible impulsion, and the tiniest of waves breaking on the edge with scarce a bubble of froth, but ever coming higher or receding in obedience to Nature's laws.

Mary Eleanor liked to see the 'bouncing' waves best. They seemed full of play and fun and naughty tricks, and so happy chasing each other up the beach, and even when they were big and boisterous and wild, they were having a great old time.

But the quiet, sullen oncoming of the waters during an easterly spell saddened her and made her think that it was like some things that happened in life. Things that had to be gone through, whether one desired them or not –

things that took their course, and that a little girl's efforts were fruitless to avoid, and things that happened in everyday life that were not pleasant to experience but inevitable, and had as surely to be endured as the tide would ebb and flow twice daily.

She had been told the story of the inundated country that lay beneath the waters of Cardigan Bay and had listened with avidity to the tales and legends told of Cantre'r Gwaelod and Taliesin, and pondered over them, especially when during exceptionally low tides, a few old stumps of trees were visible, thus yielding evidence of the truth of the old tales.

She wished the surrounding old hills could tell tales of the centuries long past, and wondered if there were little girls then who played on a seashore now many miles out to sea under deep waters, and who watched the ocean with a similar fascination to her own.

But these were daydreams that were seldom carried to their conclusion, for invariably they were broken into by a call to little household duties which she was capable of performing, unless she had been given an hour or two for playing on the beach and her time was her own.

She was one of those fortunate children who enjoyed playing by herself as much as with little friends, and could quite pleasurably pass the time away by herself on the beach if no playmate were near.

She often indulged in a thinking spell, as she called it, if playing alone. Now when Mary Eleanor had one of her thinking spells, she invariably tried to find a quiet spot that would ensure privacy and an uninterrupted time for this important business, until she chose to put her serious-minded spell aside, or else had solved the problem which for the time being appeared to call for undivided attention, in order to arrive at a satisfying solution, and the beach had often proved such a spot.

She never liked to find that she had not brought to bear on the subject both personal and impersonal views. 'Suppose I do want it' and 'Suppose I don't want it' were the questions she put to herself as she pondered over the complexity of some of her little life's conundrums. To each of these questions she would put further negative and positive objections and suggestions until at times, her very wits grew muddled, and she would exclaim to herself impatiently, 'I wish I had a brain sponge! The slate of my brain is covered up full with thoughts and figures, so that I can't think another thought clearly. Oh, dear! I must leave it for another time.'

Thus wisely leaving the enigmas she could not solve until a more propitious time arrived, she would throw herself wholeheartedly into the next in order, be it games, schoolwork, meals or small errands.

She tried to avoid being very quiet or serious unless occupied with her homework for school, as her little periods of reverie were frequently the forerunners of a dose of camomile tea (or worse still a combination of camomile and wormwood tea) the next morning. She never relished this dose that was to ensure a clear tongue and head and had to be taken cold before her breakfast.

She generally had to reach for the bundle of camomile flowers tied up in a bag in a dry place, and, taking a few stalks with their bitter-smelling flowers from the bunch, place them in a jug ready for her aunt, thus having to sniff the objectionable stuff beforehand. It stayed about on her fingers and in the room, she fancied, for all the evening whenever she had to get it.

On pouring boiling water over the stalks a decoction was made that formed a homely remedy much used in the village for clearing the tongue and toning up the system. The addition of the wormwood made it taste so bitter and horrid that Mary Eleanor indulged in many a grimace as she tried to swallow it in gulps to avoid tasting it, and she always held the spoon of sugar quite ready to take as soon as she had got rid of the disliked potion.

In almost every house she had been in she had seen the bunches of herbs hanging up, and in some cases they certainly did not look very inviting as they were exposed to all dust arising in the room, and not covered with a bag as at her home. She supposed other children had the unpleasant drink at times.

The early spring was proving a mild one this year, and Mary Eleanor realised that she would not see any snow on the ground at all this year; each year in her home in America there had been heavy snow throughout the winter, and she had told her schoolmates a lot about their sleds and winter sports, and had mentioned sleigh rides, but she fancied that the tales she told were scarcely credited and according to her wont, ceased talking on the subject.

She found that even when it snowed in the village, it did not stay long and the children did not often get enough snow to make snowballs, much less snowmen. The only snow of the winter had been the whitened tops of the mountains around when a cold spell or two had occurred, and now spring was fast approaching.

Standing on the top of the old sea fence and looking up and down the length of the beach, Mary Eleanor could see evidence of the village preparations for the early spring cleaning, for sheets and blankets and heavy washings of curtains were laid out to dry on the clean shingle. She had herself helped to lay small stones on her aunt's washing spread on the stony part of the beach to keep the wind from blowing them away.

The clothes dried both quickly and sweetly thus laid out and were quickly got out of the way in the fine weather which prevailed. Carpets and mats of all descriptions were the next items in the annual village upheaval, and early and late the housewives vied with each other in the amount of work done. As the sun grew warmer each day, mattresses began to make their appearance and these were subjected to a beating that must have wearied the arms of the workers and were turned and aired and sweetened by the fresh sea breezes and sun. Mending and cleaning and house papering and painting went on with great vigour, and Mary Eleanor quite enjoyed the beeswaxy smell in the houses where the yearly agitation due to the great spring ceremonial was near its end.

Fresh leaves were pushing out all over the ivy by the front door and bachelor's buttons and gilly flowers peeping up in the diminutive front garden, and the village preened itself in readiness for the expected influx of summer visitors, who were a great source of income to the villagers.

CHAPTER 2

MARY ELEANOR PUTS AWAY CHILDISH THINGS, AND BECOMES...

Rain! Rain yesterday, and the day before, and all the week before, and still it rained!

Where it had all been stored in the great blue sky was a source of wonder to Mary Eleanor as she looked out at the leaden sky in the west that lowered its grey masses of rainclouds down to the distant horizon where it appeared to invisibly join an equally leaden sea, sullen and swollen in its turbulent, unceasing writhing and tossing with an occasional 'white horse' of foam in the far distance that Mary Eleanor had learned to associate with the rising of a gale.

Grey skies and grey days made one feel that colour, she thought as she stood watching the heaving billows. When a child of tender years is left much to her own thoughts in between the busy and fully occupied hours of play and work in school, there is developed in that child a trend of thought and feeling centred mainly on the why and wherefore of things in the universe, and Mary Eleanor's inquisitive and ever-active brain dwelt largely on Nature's many and varied changes.

With no playmates excepting during the hours of school and a brief time after hours, she had learned to depend on herself for company, and occupied herself in a wholehearted manner by taking an interest in a number of things little dreamed of by those in whose care she had been placed.

Just now, she was pondering over the sermon preached on the preceding Sabbath and its apparent direct bearing upon a subject which greatly exercised her mind at present. Naturally of an open and trusting temperament, Mary Eleanor held that no minister of the Gospel would ever dare to say things that were not true, and believed implicitly any or all statements made by them.

Consequently any text expounded by the preachers in the little seaside village chapel on the Sabbath was always taken to heart as directly applicable to herself.

So simple and yet so earnest was her faith that she often fancied God made the preacher choose his text as being the very one she needed to solve a vexing question which had, perhaps, been puzzling her little soul in the preceding week, and as the preacher waxed more and more fervid at times in his delivery as he worked himself up to the utmost pitch of what her elders designated the 'hywl', she felt that the appeal in the sermon was directly to her.

And now as she gazed out over the broad grey waters from her bedroom window, she decided that the former Sabbath's sermon *must* have been preached to fit her case, the text being 'When I became a man, I put away childish things.'

She had been urged continually during the last few months 'to be a woman, not to be childish', and though she had a child's longing to play with toys and things that belonged to

Childhood's realm, she was frequently chidden for her fondness of them until the child heart of her shrank sensitively from the censure and she began to take herself to task for not 'growing up' in feeling and keeping pace with her rapid bodily growth.

'If I don't play with my dolly, what am I to do with her? What is she good for but to play with? I can sew dresses for her, and I can wash her clothes, and keep her tidy, and I'm tired of reading the two books here,' she soliloquised. 'Anyway, I'll make dolly comfortable for tonight', and turning away from her long contemplation of the grey sea, she climbed the few stairs to the corner of the attic where she was allowed to keep her 'trash', as her few little treasures were called.

The dolly so loved by her had been the gift of those who were far away across that big sea that held her fascinated so frequently as her child mind tried to grasp the immensity of it, and the length of the distance separating her from the very ones who had sewn the doll's clothes, and knitted her bonnet, and made them all to 'put on and off' so that Mary Eleanor could dress and undress her treasure whenever she pleased.

She had thought that she would play with her doll for years and years, and now she had grown to feel half ashamed of saying that she was going upstairs to play with her doll, as she was so often told that big girls like her did not play with dolls but tried to be little women.

It was with a sorely tried mind that she took up her doll from the box where she always laid it covered over with a clean duster, and newspaper on top to keep it 'tidy' and laid her gently on the floor while she turned over, in thoughtful mood, the small treasures that were placed in the lower part of the box.

There were odd lengths of gaily flowered silks, diminutive bits of lace, some soft pliable scraps of velvet, muslins and embroideries; coming across a little needle-book with a few lengths of sewing cotton, she put it into her small workbox, which was kept by the box of toys.

Turning over the articles slowly, she arrived at a possible solution to her problem as she resolved to 'spring clean' all the little bits of velvet, silk, and muslin by a vigorous brushing and careful folding away in the box as tidily as possible.

Among the debris in the old attic she had found an ancient reticule long since past its day and yet which she had been pleased to add to her treasures as a 'pretend' travelling bag.

Mary Eleanor, having once made up her mind over a problem, never hesitated to carry it out, and now, jumping up from the box and its untidy contents, she ran downstairs for a tiny whisk brush, and when asked what she was going to do with it, burst out with 'I think I'll do what the preacher told us about last Sunday. I'm growing up now, and he said when we grow up we must put away childish things, and so I thought I'd tidy dolly up and brush her clothes and her hair and wrap her up and put her away, and if I put her away and wrap her up tightly, it will be too much trouble to open up the parcel often and so I shall not play with her so much!' And without waiting for a reply, she hastened upstairs to her contemplated occupation in case she might be tempted to change her mind.

Disrobing the waxen-faced doll, she tenderly brushed from it a few specks of sawdust that had somehow worked out through the loosely stitched joints, and one by one replaced the handmade articles that her little girl friends had kindly sewn so neatly from the scraps given her by a Boston dressmaker just before she had come across that big sea.

The little lace-trimmed underwear was soon put on and tied and buttoned with special care and the pale blue cashmere dress with its pretty frilled sleeves, which completed dolly's wardrobe, fastened with the tiniest of white glove buttons, was given a final pull and gentle patting into place, and then the doll's hair brushed gently before the blue woollen hood was tied on.

Seeing a speck of dust in the eyes, Mary Eleanor screwed up a wisp of muslin, gently poked it around the staring optics with a loving touch, then laid the doll down on her lap, and addressing it in her quaint way, she said, 'Now, dolly, I've had some real good times with you, but they are beginning to make fun of me, because I play with you. I don't mind that, I could stand being laughed at for your sake, but I am not pleasing them, for they say I am growing up to be a big girl now and must not be childish any longer. I *must* do what they tell me, for I promised I would, and so, dolly dear, I've dressed you and made you tidy for the last time, and I'm going to wrap you up tight and cosy and put you in this reticule. I shall not forget you, and sometimes I'll come and pat the reticule gently and you'll know I'm near. But I won't open it, because I shall want to see you again, if I do, and so I am going to put you away until next year, and then I can see you again, because I shall want to 'spring clean' you and see that all is well; I know it's hard for you, dolly, but I understand now that the minister must have been giving me advice about the matter last Sunday, when he so often said we were to put away childish things, and if I put you away like this, I shall be pleasing everybody but myself and you. Goodbye, dolly, for one long, long year.'

Solemnly kissing the waxen face of the unresponsive doll, Mary Eleanor picked up a triangular piece of quaint grey silk with richly woven flowers of violet hue and wrapped it over the pale blue cashmere dress and woollen hood.

Then a sheet of soft tissue paper was wrapped over the silk, and a piece of newspaper carefully placed around that and the whole securely tied with white string.

Placing the doll lengthwise in the old reticule without hesitation, Mary Eleanor hung it up on a nail on one of the crossbeams of the attic, gave the hanging reticule a soft gentle patting and, as was characteristic of her, turned determinedly away, and tidied up her corner of nondescript pieces of silks, muslins, and velvets and took the whisk brush downstairs, telling her aunt that she had put dolly carefully away for a year in the old reticule and hung it up on the beam 'for tidiness', and now she would try to grow up and not be childish again and then perhaps she would be a better girl.

The infliction of self-denial invariably put Mary Eleanor in a good mood, and the net result of the virtue emanating from her self-imposed martyrdom made her thoughtful for her elders and watchful for any occasion on which she might prove herself growing up and becoming a little woman.

Consequently, such things as the distasteful daily dusting of the front room were undertaken without a demur because she had 'put away childish things'.

It was quite a few months after Mary Eleanor had so determinedly and wholeheartedly deprived herself of the companionship of her much-loved doll, that she had an overpowering desire to see her and handle fondly the little clothes and 'think over things' as she expressed it, and one Saturday afternoon after her little household duties had been performed, she went to the attic to satisfy her yearning.

She found that the general position of things in the old attic had been altered and things had been moved about and cleaned up. Consequently, when she found that the old reticule no longer hung on the nail on the crossbeam, she had no misgivings or qualms of fear about it.

Knowing instinctively that it would not do to turn things about too much, she looked around carefully for the reticule and searched in her own particular corner by the stairs but could not find it.

Realising that the article as hung on the nail was not an ornament and would help to make the place untidy – a condition abhorred by her elders – she imagined that it had been put away somewhere for the sake of 'tidiness' a word she sometimes disliked very much.

Slowly she turned around in the old attic and wondered where it could have been put. There were huge white canvas bags and old sea chests packed full of winter-weight blankets and clothes and pushed back under the eaves, but she could not see the old leather reticule and give it the loving reassuring patting she had promised dolly she would sometimes indulge in.

Giving up her search, Mary Eleanor went down the first flight of stairs to her little bedroom, and gazed out over the sea, seeking a solution to her vexing problem. She was thinking things over and trying to decide what she should do about it. If she went to ask her aunt where it had been put, she would have to endure a few minutes of questioning from which she shrank and which would perhaps include the usual reproof about her clinging to childish things as dolls and suchlike nonsense.

Yet the longing to know just where her treasure had been put away was too great, and she decided it would not be so hard to bear any reference to her shortcomings as it would be to remain in utter ignorance of the whereabouts of the reticule and its contents.

Going down to her aunt, Mary Eleanor said, in as casual a manner as she could summon under the circumstances, 'Please, Aunt, do you know where the old leather bag is where I put my doll?'

'Oh, I expect it's up there somewhere,' was the reply.

'I hung it up "tidy" on the nail, but I can't find it anywhere,' said Mary Eleanor.

'Don't you go pulling things out of their places to look for it, when I've been so hard worked cleaning up that place,' came the warning.

'No, Aunt, I have not touched anything there, but I thought you might know where the bag is. Can I have it, please, if you are not too busy to tell me where it is?' Mary Eleanor asked anxiously.

'I can't leave my work now, child, to get it for you. You must wait until another day.' And the child had to be content for the time with this reply.

Slowly for Mary Eleanor did that day and the ensuing week pass until the next Saturday dawned, and once more the little girl climbed the attic stairs to search for the reticule. All around the old four-poster bed and among the many tied-up bags and boxes did she continue her unavailing search, and finally gave up her quest and sat down by her box of sewing bits in a disconsolate manner.

'It's raining again today, and I have no one to play with. I know my Holiday Book stories by heart, and I don't want to read any more about the *Antelope* and the Pelew Islands, and Smiles' Self Help is heavy, and I can understand no more than the pictures in the Welsh books, and I don't know what to do. Oh, dear! I wish Aunt would let me have my doll for a little while!'

And, with a sigh of pity for herself, she went aimlessly downstairs to the living room.

Sitting down moodily by the table, she was told to get a book and read, but replied that she had read the two books so many times she knew what was on the next page all the time, and was tired of them.

'Goodness sake, child, find something to do, then, and don't sit there idling.'

'Can you please find my doll's bag this afternoon, if you are not too busy,' she queried.

'No, I can't be bothered to look for that old thing today. Don't worry me all the time about it. Go and do some patchwork,' was the reply given to the anxious enquirer.

Rising and once more going up to her secluded corner on the attic stairs, she commenced to pull her pieces of velvet and silk from the box and tried to concentrate her mind on the, at present, uninspiring task of making a patchwork cushion cover.

But Mary Eleanor's interest did not hold and the heavy downpour of rain on the roof, which would have held for her a silvery musical note had she been pleasantly occupied with her dolly, had a depressive effect on her in her present mood. She thought it was unjust that she should be debarred from seeing her doll when she had so faithfully and conscientiously carried out her part. She reasoned that she did not want to play with it, only look at it, and her little heart seemed overflowing with just the longing to handle once more those neatly trimmed little garments so much finer and nicer than anything she had seen among her school friends, who were always making coarse Welsh flannel underclothes for themselves or members of their families.

She had an innate appreciation of fine things that was rare in a child and the texture of a piece of velvet, cloth, or silk of good quality called for her admiration and approbation. She loved to handle the soft pile of the velvet or smooth her fingers over the glossy surface of a piece of good satin with a loving touch.

Some day – that day in the future of all children's dreams – everything she had would be made of marvellous velvets and silks.

Just at this moment, however, a longing for the fine blue cashmere dress of her doll was in the ascendant, and as she selected tiny patch after patch of silk or velvet and laid them together to plan out a cushion of hexagonal bits of varied colours, she could not keep her mind intent on the matching of colours, and finally in despair, she gathered all together and threw them into the box in a disgusted manner and again went downstairs, uncertain of her next movements.

'I see you forgot to dust the front room this morning, Mary Eleanor. Go and get a duster and do it. Someone will come in to tea tomorrow and I shall be ashamed of the room if it is not dusted,' said her aunt.

Going obediently to the duster drawer, she took up a soft clean duster, and found courage to say inquiringly as she went through the door, 'I can have my doll after I've done it, please, for a little while, can I? If you are not too busy?' she added apologetically.

'Bother that old doll of yours! I thought you'd got tired of it by now. No, you can't have it, for it isn't there!' came the unexpected reply.

'Isn't there? Why, I put it safe myself on the nail!' exclaimed Mary Eleanor in astonishment, coming back into the room.

'You are too old now to bother with such rubbish, and I got rid of it when I cleaned the attic out the other week,' retorted her aunt.

With slow emphasis on each word, Mary Eleanor repeated, 'You – got – rid – of – my – doll?'

'Yes, it would only harbour moths and looked untidy, so I burned it and got rid of it. Go on now and do your dusting,' was added as Mary Eleanor, stunned by what was to her a dire tragedy, turned away and closed the door, incapable of any further comment, and went into the front room. But not to dust! Oh, no!

Standing inside the door, she repeated slowly to herself in an undertone between clenched teeth, 'She DARED to burn my doll! She dared to BURN my doll! MINE! She had no right to do that. It was MINE! It is burned! Oh! OH! I hate her, I hate her! I'll never do anything she wants me to do again. Dust her old things! I'll smash up everything that I can break in this room. I hate her, I want my doll, I want my doll's clothes. *THERE*'s your old duster on the floor. See me stand on it! I'm mad with you. You wicked, wicked woman. I'll run away. Oh! I don't care what becomes of me. I've tried to be a good girl, and now I'm going to be as wicked as I can be. I'm never going to be a good girl anymore for anyone! It will serve her right. It was my doll, and I had been a good girl about it and had put it away, and I trusted her. I'll never believe another word she says. Oh, she was wicked, and she has broken my heart. I'd got nothing much else to love here, and now it's gone. She had so much, and I so little and she actually burned my doll! I'm wicked now, I know I am, and I am never going to be anything else. I'm mad with her. How could she be so cruel? All those pretty little clothes burned! Oh, my doll!'

Scarcely knowing what she did, with never a tear from those eyes bright and shining in the intensity of the storm of passion that shook her, she picked up the duster from beneath her feet, swished it around the legs of the table, and over a shelf or two, looked at the mantelpiece an instant, and then with meticulous care dusted the shells and clock and vases with pendulous prisms, and with a final flick over the fender, went out of the front room in a dazed, maddened mood.

Taking the duster up to her room, she noticed that the rain had ceased, and she hurriedly put on an old hat of hers, ran downstairs, saying as she passed the living room door, 'I'm going for a walk. It has stopped raining.' And without waiting for permission, as was her wont, went out into the road and ran swiftly towards the field beyond the railroad crossing.

She was going where no one could see her; like a wounded animal hiding its hurt, she fled from the vicinity of any person or persons likely to speak to her, until she reached a small disused quarry on the riverbank where she knew she would be uninterrupted, and unseen. Flinging herself down on the slaty shingle scarcely dry from the rain, she gave vent to a torrent of tears that brought relief to her overladen little heart.

Long she lay there, grieving as she had not done for many a long day, and it was not until she began to feel tired of her position that she sat up and looked out over the river in the near distance to the fields beyond.

Her sobs gradually lessened as the chaotic state of her mind subsided and settled down into a reasoning and explaining time.

Feeling utterly friendless and alone, she felt exhausted by the very intensity of her grief and it was a stunned and bruised-hearted child that rose from the slaty shingle and went slowly down to the riverside to bathe her swollen eyelids and remove traces of her tears. She had truly put away childish things, and had become ...?

She had had one of life's hardest knocks, in that a trust had been betrayed and a child's tender, simple faith had been shaken to its very foundations. Never in after life would she be able to believe in full confidence and implicit faith as she had formerly, what her elders chose to say. She realised dimly that she had grieved her Heavenly Father and humbly went back to the little quarry and kneeling down asked God to tell her what to do and to please wipe off from His recording slate all her naughty words and her bad temper. She had forgotten how to be good for a little while, but He knew how much she had wanted her doll and the little clothes and so He would be sorry enough to forgive her for her awful tantrum.

Comforted by her action, she slowly went homewards, occasionally stopping to pick fresh green fronds that looked so delicate and lacy among the bracken-covered patches of field down by the riverside, and that would look so pretty with the fresh golden gorse that grew in such profusion nearby.

The scent of gorse, freshened by the clean rain, pleased her and made her load her little hands with its bloom to take home, and as she gathered the fragrant blossoms with their 'prickly defenders' as she called them, her heart gradually eased itself of its burden, and the child, as forgiving as she felt forgiven, took the flowers home to be placed in one of the many old-fashioned Welsh jugs on the dresser as a mute peace offering.

CHAPTER 3

MARY ELEANOR'S 'YARN CURE'

Something seemed to be radically wrong with Mary Eleanor. Nothing seemed to claim her attention for long. She had lost her usual hearty appetite and was quite finicky over the food placed before her at any meal of the day; her listlessness was causing many a surmise and conjecture about its origin, and she was frequently asked whether she had any headache or pain or any sore feeling anywhere. If not, why not join with her schoolmates in their play? She replied that she did not feel like it, and she was quite well, thank you. Well, then, would it not be nice to go for a walk to fetch home the butter and its accompanying tin bottle of buttermilk?

This was an errand that generally appealed to Mary Eleanor, as she was fond of watching the animals she saw at the farm not far from the village and from which the weekly supply of butter was obtained.

But today it was in a half-hearted manner that Mary Eleanor fell in with this suggestion, and perfunctorily got the basket with its clean napery for covering the pound of butter which sometimes had a swan moulded on the top and sometimes a cow. She had often carefully turned back the clean napkin to gaze in wonder on cow or swan, and envy the possessor of the clever hand that had carved them out. The cow's legs always seemed so very fine and thin, and she very much admired the pretty curve in the neck of the swan.

It was a matter of wonder to her how they always managed to be exactly the same. She had never witnessed the process of butter-making, and many an hour had passed swiftly away on the sandy beach as she tried to make what would look like pats of butter out of the sand and seawater.

Dry sand would not cohere, and sand that was too wet would not stay in shape. She had learned to get the sand and water of the right consistency to press into a handle-less cup she had found thrown away on the beach, so that it would turn out cup-shape, but it never seemed to be just right enough to respond to her gentle manipulations as she tried with almost illimitable patience to make a cow or swan on the top of the shape.

Having the basket with clean cloth inside in which, very carefully wrapped in a fragment of newspaper and safely tucked away in its folds, was the usual shilling and varying odd pence to pay for the butter, Mary Eleanor fetched the large tin bottle – which was so easily taken to the farm, but which made her arms ache with the weight of buttermilk ere she reached home – and started off on her errand.

It was an errand she had always enjoyed, but today she did not know what she wanted or liked. She wondered why the antics of the tadpoles in the shallow water in the ditch by the roadside were not so funny as usual; they were quite too fat and lazy for the wiggly contortions they had amused her with last time she had passed them, and thus, with her step lacking its customary sprightliness, she meandered along the road to the farm, taking far less than her habitual interest in Nature's little comedies and sideshows.

Although warm, it was not a very hot day, and she could not, in consequence, expect her homeward burden of buttermilk to grow any less as was frequently the case when a passing neighbour requested a draught of the refreshing liquid, if the day proved sultry; she reflected that she might enjoy it better if only folks would not take such liberties – she had learned that it would never do to refuse the request.

She had never been able to accustom herself to the kind of noonday meal that invariably followed the fresh supply of buttermilk. It seemed marvellous to her that anyone could sit down and enjoy most heartily, even smacking lips the while, the frugal meal of hot mashed potatoes and buttermilk.

She could enjoy, and frequently took, a drink of the fresh buttermilk with its slightly acid flavour, but begged to be preserved from having to drink it after the first day of churning; she knew her dinner would be the mashed potatoes spread on bread and butter with a cup of tea, and very possibly, a boiled egg. But as the latter very often formed part of her breakfast, it was seldom that a second could be afforded the same day, unless eggs were at their cheapest.

She had the cheering prospect of the rapidly approaching summer holiday from school, and she hoped to spend many a sunny morning on the beach, and she mentally determined that she would gather enough winkles and limpets to supply her with a relish on the days the inevitable mashed potatoes and buttermilk formed the staple article of diet at noon.

It may be that it was because she was 'too finicky' as they said, that she did not care for some of the Welsh dishes. She had often tried to overcome her dislike, if only to obtain freedom from remarks that made her feel squirmy all over and want to answer back; this she felt would be rude and disrespectful.

There were times when she became painfully self-conscious of her failings and this made her face grow uncomfortably warm and the food in her mouth became very awkward to masticate and a crumb would persist in getting where it should not be, and finally she would have to indulge in a sort of choking cough to clear matters.

Noting her confusion, her elders generally changed the subject, and the disliked article of diet was removed from her place at the table and something more to her liking substituted.

Musing on such matters, the journey to the farm was accomplished, the butter promptly put in her basket, this time neatly put on a saucer and covered with a fresh cabbage leaf as the weather had been rather warm and the butter inclined to be soft and oily.

Handing the basket and bottle of buttermilk to the child, the farmer's wife asked her if she would like a drink of milk. This kind offer was eagerly accepted by Mary Eleanor as a rare treat. No nectar ever quaffed tasted better than the occasional glass of fresh milk she sometimes got at the farm – milk that was so thick and creamy that she always tried to drain the very last drop out of the glass.

On one memorable occasion she had been given a small bottle of fresh milk to carry home as well for her supper, and although it made the basket a bit heavy, she willingly carried it, remarking that it balanced the buttermilk better and added, naively, that it would be a good plan to bring a similar bottle each time even if she only filled it with water, as it would make equal weights almost, so one side would not get tired sooner than the other, at the same time accompanying her remarks with an innocent glance upwards at the kindly face of the farmer's wife.

The latter, feeling that such an ingenuous statement called for her personal approval, told Mary Eleanor that if she remembered to bring the small glass bottle with her each time, she could have it filled and filled with the best milk. 'And if I am not here to do it for you, child, ask the maid for it, saying I told you to do so.' As Mary Eleanor demurely said, 'Thank you very much,' and took her leave, she turned aside to her husband and excused her action by remarking that there was something so quaint and irresistible about the child with her big thoughtful eyes that she felt compelled to give her the milk in return for her very nice manners and frank way of replying to any remark of hers.

Cheered by the kindness of the farmer's wife, and hoping that she would be allowed to have all the milk in the bottle for her own use, and not have to put it on the table to share with others in order that a pint less might be purchased from the milkman next morning,

Mary Eleanor set off homeward. She decided that the farm lady was one of those people that one could never forget, because they had been kind, and she told herself that when she grew up, she would make it her especial duty to find out little girls' needs and wants that were not always talked about but just longed for in their little hearts.

Now she knew of lots of little things that would make her very happy, but her elders decidedly disapproved of some of them when they were ever so carefully and guardedly approached on such matters, and so, of course, there were other little desires that one felt were too sacred to talk about. Such innocent cravings were instinctively concealed in the inner chambers of her small brainbox and not discussed, except in her own self-communings.

Ever loyal to her own people, Mary Eleanor would not have spoken a word in censure of them to anybody. Nay, rather, had anyone at any time been indiscreet enough to say anything that might be construed as uncomplimentary to them, she would at once have found a ready reply, which invariably made them pause and pacify her by contradicting in a convincing manner their former openly expressed opinion.

She excused her relatives to herself at times by endeavouring to impress on her mind that they had quite forgotten just how much a little girl could long for a thing, because so many long years had passed since they were children themselves. She hoped God would always keep her heart quite like a little girl's, so that she'd remember when she grew old just how a little girl felt sometimes.

Placing the basket containing the butter on a grassy hummock on the shady side of the roadside, she stood the heavy milk can carefully in a little depression near it and sat down to rest her arms.

Nature, in any phase, appealed strongly to her little soul and as her eyes took in the deep purple of the background of Welsh hills, just across the river beyond the stretch of bogland, she smiled at the beautiful peaceful picture and recalled the fact that she had been promised a day somewhere on the bog picking cranberries and bilberries while peat was being piled up in a stack after drying ready for carrying home on the back in a huge Welsh basket called a cawell.

She had happened to say one day that she liked cranberry sauce and had asked if there were any in Wales, and blueberries! Why, they were nicer than all the blackberries that ever grew.

After a little discussion, it was concluded that both of the much-longed-for berries grew on the bogland, and one day they were going to get some.

The kind farmer's wife had made her think of Hannah Berry in some indefinite way, and Aunt Han's blueberry biscuits, light as air, made with cream and whitest of flour and blueberries which spilt all over in luscious rich purple juice when one bit into the hot delicacy and drank unlimited quantities of milk for breakfast, with an appetite sharpened by a run over the pastures in the early morning on a barefoot chase driving the milking cows to the far meadow.

What a long time ago that seemed, and yet it was only the summer before! She supposed she must be growing up and so lots of different things had been happening to her that year and now, instead of watching the cheeky chipmunk race along the stone walls of the fields and disappear chattering and scolding at the approach of noisy playmates, she was watching the sun cast a rosy glamour over the bogland, magically blending with richest purple in the mountainous background against which the seagulls' wings gleamed silvery-white as they wheeled and turned and flew in utter abandon over the distant estuary.

Feeling that she had stayed long enough for her first rest, she picked up her burdens and started once more toward home, brightened and heartened by the scene spread before her by munificent Nature.

For the latter part of her journey, the road home lay parallel with the beach, and she thought it would be pleasant to take her next rest on the clean dry shingle before going on to the wet sandy beach, which the fast-ebbing tide was leaving unsullied and untrodden. The rest of the distance home would pass pleasantly enough by leaving traces on the sand of her progress by short step, wide step, long step, and close step, a game she had invented to make the errand pleasanter.

She would have to avoid the wettest part of the beach in order to make clear impressions, and she would not have to soak her boots so thickly with olive oil (a task she disliked immensely) if she took the higher almost dry part of the beach.

Reaching the shingle, Mary Eleanor carefully picked her way with due consideration for the saucer of butter until she almost reached the sandy beach before she sat down, congratulating herself that she had evaded, without seeming intent, that funny talkative woman who was approaching on the road from the village just as she took to the pebbly stretch between the road and the beach.

Depositing her basket in her shadow, lest the sun might make the butter too soft and the trouble consequently attributed to her leisurely homecoming, she sat down for her second rest and watched the receding tide's murmuring wavelets breaking one over the other so gently, each one creeping up a shorter distance than the one before, while little sandpipers followed the ebbing waters and gorged themselves with whatever dainty appealed to their fancy among the flotsam and jetsam left by the outgoing tide. She had always been fascinated by the sea – she had seen it in many moods in the past year, and had never tired of watching its ever-varying ebb and flow.

Blue of sea and blue of sky seemed to unite and blend on the horizon in such a perfect manner as she watched it that she recalled the purple of the mountains she had admired a little earlier on her way home, and thought God must be very clever to make use of such rich shades of colour without getting any smudgy results such as she got when she tried to mix the ultramarine and Prussian blue on the palette of her crude little paintbox at home in an endeavour to get a colour that looked just like the sky in summer.

Perhaps as she grew up she would learn how great painters could copy the wonderful sky so well, and she thought they surely would have to work quickly when copying, for God's sky never looked the same very long – it was so continually changing.

Those great big rosy-white clouds to the north end of the beach altered their shape every instant; at one minute she might fancy there were huge flocks of sheep depicted, the next, the very clouds she watched seemed pulled about by invisible strings and mountains of snow would appear, to alter and contort themselves in turn into faces and animals, continents and islands, indeed almost anything one could think of as one watched, and all done so quietly and mysteriously. That was one thing that made God so much greater than the greatest painter.

At last, rested by her stay on the pebbly edge of the beach, she stood up with her basket and bottle and began her careful placing of steps, chanting in an undertone the while, the order – short step, wide step, long step, close step – her eyes on the sand, stopping only once or twice to look back over her track to see if she took a straight line.

Finding that she appeared to get nearer the shingle at times while at others she tended outwards to the sea, she smiled to herself as she sighted a prominent piece of one of the old sea-groynes, and knew she could correct the crooked line by keeping a distant permanent goal in view. Thus progressing, she reached her home, and clambered up the old sea fence and its makeshift ladders to the backyard of the house.

Whether it was that the journey and the heat had tired her, she did not know; she had been glad to go to her little bedroom for some nights now and on this night she felt very tired and so, saying she was sleepy, went upstairs soon to be lost in dreamless slumber.

As she dressed next morning, her aunt came into the room, fingering a piece of coarse oily grey Welsh yarn, like the yarn that some of the girls in school used for knitting stockings on sewing afternoons.

This yarn had a peculiar odour which she disliked, and she always tried to avoid sitting next to a girl who was obliged to knit with this yarn. She had been asked once to help pick up some stitches dropped in such a stocking and she noticed how the coarse yarn left a peculiar greasiness on the needles that made it hard to slip the stitches on and off. It was wonderful, she thought, to see the quick way some of the girls could knit with this coarse yarn.

The stockings she had to knit were of thick black wool and it did not smell at all objectionable. The mere handling of the greasy yarn made her wipe her fingers hard on her pinafore to get rid of the greasiness which otherwise would have got on her own knitting needles and her stitches in consequence would stick and squeak, making her shiver and setting things on edge generally.

'Before you put on your dress, child, I want to tie this on your arm,' was the reply when Mary Eleanor asked her aunt what she was going to do with the yarn. Thinking it was a joke of some sort, she laughed and said, 'I've got a spare piece of black wool with my knitting, if you want to measure my arm. I'll get that ...'

'No, no,' was the reply. 'You know you have not been very well lately—'

'Why! I'm not sick!' Mary Eleanor laughingly interrupted.

'No, not exactly,' answered her aunt, 'but people keep saying how quiet you are, and there is sometimes a little sickness of that sort that a thing like this cures.'

Amused beyond expression at the thought, Mary Eleanor got her knitting bag and the piece of black wool and said, 'This is cleaner than that old piece. Tie this on.'

'No, that won't do. I asked Anne Jenkins about it last night, and she said that if I gave her husband a shilling, he would measure the yarn necessary and pray over it, and that is what this is. You are to have it tied tightly on the left arm high up, and after a week or so, it will act and make you better. As you get better it will slip down your arm so that you can't keep it up and then we can take it off,' explained her aunt.

'Why didn't the man use wool that was nice and clean like my black wool?' Mary Eleanor queried.

'I don't know; it is part of the cure to have the yarn straight from the weaver's hank and not even rolled into a ball. Then he cuts a length and stretches it out and prays over it and it shortens up somehow, they say, and holds the healing power that cures you. Come, let me put it on.'

Mary Eleanor submitted with a grimace and the yarn was duly tied in place; she declared that she would smell its disagreeable odour so long as she had to wear it, and that people would know she'd got it on.

'Not unless you yourself tell them, Mary Eleanor,' was the reply, 'and I cannot afford another shilling to Anne Jenkins' husband for another piece. If you tell people, it will not do you any good. Be a good girl and remember what I have told you and you'll soon be better.' The child was left to complete her dressing.

Looking at the grey strands of wool tied tightly in place on her arm, in utter disgust she slipped her school dress on over the offending object, and with a muddle of thoughts striving for foremost place in her little head, went to her breakfast.

Beside her porridge plate was the remainder of the milk she had failed to drink the night before because she had been too tired, and this she enjoyed, following it up with bread and butter. Getting her things together, she went to school, after solemnly asking her aunt when a quiet chance occurred whether the yarn would make her arm sore, as it itched very much already. Receiving a reply in the negative and an assurance that it might be loosened a little in the dinner hour if it still felt irritable, she appeared reconciled to the perplexing and crude charm against a sickness which she did not have as far as she knew.

She was absent-minded and preoccupied to an unusual extent, and her teacher asked her at last whether she had a headache since she did not pay attention to her lessons. This roused her for a brief while and she tried to concentrate on whatever lesson was proceeding.

Quick at figures, she always had a lot of time to spare when working her arithmetic examples, and this morning she rapidly finished her work, and then tried to reason out the why and wherefore of the yarn. She recalled the whispered conversations between her relatives and Anne Jenkins in the preceding days, accompanied by occasional covert glances in her direction, and now knew what had been the subject under discussion. But she could not make out the connection between God's healing power and the dirty grey wool, prayed over though it had been by a chapel deacon.

Why could not God bless a few strands of clean white cotton or wool quite as well as that filthy yarn? Of course, it might be one of the ways of subduing the flesh and making one more meek and submissive by having to put on things one did not like the look or smell of and which made one feel creepy-crawly. Thus, in a ceaseless round of conjecture and with no apparent solution to the numerous vexatious problems that puzzled her, the morning passed away.

She was asked whether she had told anyone about the yarn, and answered that it was not a thing she would like to talk about because the girls all knew how much she disliked the Welsh yarn they used for knitting stockings and she could smell the yarn all the time now, but hoped to get rid of it in about ten days as had been promised.

As her arm grew accustomed to the feel of the tight yarn, she gradually forgot it, and it was only when she undressed at night that she noticed it at all, and then it worried her because it left a rather dirty greasy mark which took good hard rubbing to clean off, and she felt compelled to add to her prayers the petition that God would please excuse the yarn if it did not please Him, as she could not very well refuse to wear it.

The school holidays would commence in a few days and she thought it possible to keep the secret that long, for one of the three days left of school was a sewing day; the smell of the girls' own knitting would conveniently cover any offending odour from her small piece.

One thing that comforted her and eased her martyrdom a little was the fact that some of the girls declared they liked the smell of the yarn, while some said that they were not aware of any difference in their yarn and Mary Eleanor's wool except the colour.

She reasoned also that probably the Welsh girls were so inured to the peculiar odour of the yarn in their own homes that they did not notice it, since every wife and mother knitted the supply of socks and stockings needed in the family during the long winter evenings spent around the peat fires in neighbourly gossip in the semi-darkness, the occasional lighting of a 'canwyll frwynen' (rush-light) for a dropped stitch being all that was necessary for illumination.

She could hear the rapid click-click of the needles in fancy now as she remembered sitting on a low three-legged stool during the previous winter listening to tales that varied from local gossip and its many and, at times, heated discussions to weird stories that made Mary Eleanor's flesh creep as she listened spellbound to things that had happened to this or the other member of the group and the truth of which was invariably vouched for in solemn tones by each narrator.

It was after a few days of uncomplaining submission to the presence of the yarn that Mary Eleanor was told that a neighbour's boy had been cured of 'clefyd y galon', as it was called, by similar treatment very recently and so it was confidently expected that she would soon be alright and become brighter and happier than she had been of late, for she had obediently worn it herself, whereas the boy would have none of it.

His mother had had to wear it for him, a cure by proxy as it were, and it was because of the mother's great faith that it had proved effective. It was to be hoped that Mary Eleanor would make the cure act quickly by believing that she would soon get better and by her belief assist the cure.

As these admonitions were given in the gravest of tones, Mary Eleanor was much concerned about her own attitude toward the yarn cure and although she fancied that since she hated it so during all her waking moments she must be a very great sinner indeed, she trusted that a further addition to her evening prayer, to the effect that she was sorry it could not seem true to her, would counteract the evil, and added each night the reminder that there was one more day less on which God would have to forgive her and overlook her wrongdoing, and as soon as she could leave it off, it would be alright and there would be no more sin on account of the yarn.

Needless to say, the yarn, in the course of the week, slackened by the movement of the child's arm which continually strained it, worked down to her elbow, and gleefully she announced the fact that she could not keep it up any longer.

She was vastly relieved in mind and body when it was untied and solemnly placed in the fire. It would presumably have been sacrilege to use the piece to help out any knitting.

Her prayers that night contained an expression of thanks that God could really be friends again with her because she had no more yarn troubles to worry over and make her feel naughty, and her sleep, unbroken by dreams of failing in her duties God-ward because of necessary submission to her elders, was restful and profound.

CHAPTER 4

MARY ELEANOR AND THE BEACH

Summer holidays and freedom from school ties were eagerly anticipated by Mary Eleanor during the hot July days of that unusually fine summer. Each morning as she rose, and saw from her bedroom window the long stretch of cool firm sand between her and the sea, she thought it would be far preferable to be able to spend the long hours on the beach than to go into the old schoolroom which seemed so hot and close of late.

Putting on of shoes and stockings and tidying up for school seemed such needless duties. She had been promised that if the very nice weather lasted, she might go barefoot on the beach during the greater part of the holiday, and she awaited the coming of freedom from school hours impatiently. What knowledge she gleaned during the day she felt she could have learned in a few minutes, only she had to stay in with her classes the full school time and be 'present', and she chafed inwardly at the slow passing of the time in school.

She had read through all the school books, and watching the antics of the buzzing flies on the window, or the mischief-making tricks of a boy or girl on another form soon wearied her.

Sewing afternoons passed away without much longing, for a general quiet murmur of talk was permitted among the girls as they sewed or knitted, and Mary Eleanor never ceased to be fascinated by the tales told by the girls near her.

Their lives appeared to be so different from what hers had been in the past, and the Welsh games and ways were new to her. Sometimes she had held them entranced as she told her little stories about the Fourth of July and picnics and holidays spent in the woods by the lakes of New England, but she more often proved to be a listener to, than a recounter of, tales.

It was in a wholehearted manner that Mary Eleanor joined in the 'Hip-Hurray!' given by the children when told that school would close one day earlier than expected, and when school hours were over and the schoolchildren filed out, she joined in their merry exit shouting and laughing for sheer relief as noisily as any of them.

Scarcely staying to partake of her tea, off came the offending shoes and stockings and, grabbing a hat of sorts, she made for the beach, which seemed to welcome her as she flung herself down on the dry silvery sand near the sea fence. Digging her toes in the yielding warm sand, she watched the silvery grains sift through them for a few brief seconds, noting the golden gleam of the sand where the sun caught the sharp shining facets of each grain, and then, springing up, made her way down to the wet sand near the sea, and paddled slowly into the water as if making each step one of utter enjoyment.

It was delicious to feel the flow of warm water around her feet, and the sand was so smooth and firm that paddling in the sea promised to be a great source of pleasure.

After a few minutes in the water, she decided that it would be nice to paddle along in the warm wavelets until she reached the seaweed-covered rocks at the south end of the beach, and picking up tiny pink and white shells or smoothing out little ripplets of sand formed by the gentle undulations of the waves of the ebbing tide, she paddled along the warm stretch, her heart full of satisfaction at the pleasant times ahead of her during the next five weeks.

On arriving at the seaweed-covered rocks, she found tiny little crabs scampering away at the slightest touch on the seaweed and watched their antics, and admired the pretty sea anemones in the little pools; she had never caught any shrimps, although she had already had them as an especial relish for tea and had been initiated into the correct method of pulling off their heads and tails and getting at the morsel of pink delicacy which made their little bodies.

She scarcely recognised in the small sand-coloured crustacean reposing on the sand in the clear pool before her the appetising dainty which she had so much enjoyed.

Putting her hand into the still pool to reach for a queerly shaped little shell – presto! The tiny shrimp which she had descried had crossed in a lightning flash to the opposite side of the little pool, and she watched it settle down on the sand until it was almost indistinguishable from its surroundings.

Over there she fancied was a very big shrimp

– why, yes, it had big eyes and must be a giant shrimp. She tried to catch it, but it eluded her by its quick movement and she gave up trying to catch it by hand. Its quick dart away when she tried to catch it made her recall trying to catch baby pickerel in the little rocky streamlet that flowed by near her home in New England – one felt sure of grasping the tiny fish that kept so very still in the water that rippled so prettily over the uneven bed of the little brook; one had only to approach ever so quietly by stepping on the bigger stones and try not to jar or move one, and always keep the pickerel in the shadow of your body, and then bend down and slowly approach the unsuspecting victim's proximity with your hand in readiness for a swift thrust down upon it, and if in the meantime it had not taken itself speedily to another part of the brook and beyond your reach, there was just a slight chance of catching it, but one failed oftener than one succeeded when the attempt was made.

She gathered a few winkles from the seaweed and tried to pry loose some of the limpets that she saw, but only succeeded in getting a little amusement from watching the small pyramid-like things cling closer and tighter to the rock on which they were the instant she touched them.

A defunct starfish or two she noticed cast up by the receding tide, and poked them about and admired their shape, chuckling to herself as she thought it must be a very easy matter to find a name for a fish that was shaped so much like its name.

Tiny flatfish which she saw in the bigger pools were also easily recognised by their very shape; winkles, she supposed, had been named because of the way they pulled in their small black shelly cap in fanciful imitation of a wink when they retired inside for safety's sake.

Her hands being laden with the many treasures she had picked up, she retraced her steps along the sands, her face reflecting in its satisfied and happy mien the peace that reigned over land and sea that quiet summer evening.

Home once more to dispose of her treasures and tell of the many wonders she had seen and to willingly retire to an early rest, because she was promised the gift of a small shrimping net to catch that giant shrimp the next day.

She learned that what she had called a giant shrimp must have been a prawn, and that they were also good to eat, but that she would not find so many of them as shrimps.

A dreamless night of slumber refreshed her, and on awaking to daylight, she sprang up and dressed quickly in eager anticipation of a long unbroken day on the beach. Slipping her feet into a soft pair of slippers, she rejoiced over the absence of stockings, and gleefully kicked her feet in the air in celebration of her freedom.

The day was perfect. The sun, already high in the heavens, had warmed the smooth shingle until it almost scorched her feet, not yet hardened by exposure, and she scrambled in haste onto the cool wet sand. Seeing some white stones among the shingle, she gathered quite a little pile of them together and putting them into the old basket she had brought with her to hold her treasures, took them back to the house.

White stones were much used in the village as a border around the diminutive front gardens and she planned on using a number of them for decorative purposes in the corner of the backyard where some dwarfed and stunted shrubs (coed-y-mor) made a brave attempt at surviving the sea spray which nearly destroyed them each winter.

At any rate, she reasoned, the Tom Thumb nasturtiums with their gay red and gold blooms would look very pretty against a background of white stones from the beach. Having laboriously carried the heavy loads to place, she remembered the promised shrimping net and went into the house to see about it.

She found her aunt putting a few strengthening stitches around the hooped net, and after getting a tiny bucket in which to put some seawater so that the shrimps should not die as soon as she caught them, but be quite fresh when brought home for cooking, she thanked her aunt in her quaint way by saying she would try to catch enough shrimps to make a big meal for them both, and departed on her quest.

Her enthusiasm was checked, however, as she noticed that the shrimp pools were now covered by the incoming tide, and she had to put shrimping net and bucket away until the afternoon and content herself with building sandcastles to be washed away by the approaching sea.

She picked over the beautiful little shells she had found the day before, and cleaned the sand from the gaily hued seaweed she had gathered as treasure trove. The rich glossy brown strips looked dried up now, but the delicate red fronds of the sea fern and the white and bright green of the smaller seaweeds held their gay hues in spite of the sun's scorching rays.

Finding a brown oblong case with tail-like appendages to each corner, she was curious to know what it was, and took it to the house to be told it was what they called locally a sea-purse, and that it was the egg case of a skate. Excitedly she told of some of the queer-shaped shells she had found, and wondered how they got their different colours, some being so tiny and polished and pink, others varying from shades of grey to dark brown.

Unable to glean further information, she returned to the beach to gloat over the beauty of the tiny things and arrange them in rows and pretty devices, as she followed the happy free impulses of a true lover of Nature in her admiration of their lovely polish, colour, and diminutiveness.

Mermaids she had read of, and although realising that they were but myths and fanciful creations of the mind, she had a notion that if she were a mermaid and could live in the caves at the bottom of the sea, she would have the walls of her caves completely adorned by these delicately hued little shells in such wonderful ways that they would outshine anything ever conceived by the numerous genii attendant on Aladdin's wonderful lamp.

Having picked over the pretty shells, which had been, she knew, the homes of tiny shellfish, and put them safely in a cardboard box, she picked out the lacy bits of seaweed that retained their beauty even after drying in the hot sun and draped them over the old sea-fence to add to the beauty of her play-corner.

Finding some thick pods among the big brown bits of seaweed, she amused herself for a while by 'popping' them between two stones until called in for her midday meal.

The early afternoon passed quickly away playing 'keeping house' with a school friend, and diligently they gathered stones to mark out on the sand the plan of two- or four-roomed houses, according to their ambition, and visited each other, making great pretence at shopping and grown-up talk.

The sea, with its unfailing regularity, gradually ebbed, and when Mary Eleanor's little friend left her to go home for her little tea, an early afternoon affair in the little village, Mary Eleanor realised that by the time she had partaken of her own tea, it would be possible to indulge in the long-looked-for shrimping.

Her delight at catching a few dozen of the lively things in her net, and just one or two prawns among them, was great, and she told her aunt that the only thing she disliked about it was the wiggly way they acted as she took them from the net with her hands to put into the little bucket of seawater. They were quite prickly and she said the prawns made her feel like putting them back into the pool because they were almost too big to feel nice in her hand.

Laughingly her aunt cooked them for her by

plunging them into a saucepan of boiling water; Mary Eleanor thought it rather a cruel thing to put the lively little things straight into a boiling pot. However, it was one of the funny riddles she could not solve and as she watched the shrimps turn pink as they were plunged in the hot water she reasoned that it was a merciful and quick way since such things had to be done in order that little girls like her might get a variety of foods to eat.

She was told that since she was so fond of the beach, they would plan to picnic the next fine day on the sand dunes down by the Dovey Estuary, and pay a visit to the cockle beds there and perhaps gather a few; and thus another day was spent in the long summer sunshine, as they slowly wended their way along the lovely beach that reached from the village to the estuary in a long stretch of firm sand.

As they rounded the corner of the sandhills, Mary Eleanor saw in the near distance half-buried wrecks of old ships, some with their skeleton-like ribs standing up in solemn protest at their ignoble end, and others more sturdily defying the ravages of Time and Tide and slowly burying their old hulks in the sand in sad but sublime submission to their fate.

She listened to the stories of how the old *Providence* and the *Ellen and Mary* and the *Endeavour* and many others had been at one time the pride of the village, and the tales that were told by the winter fires later on held a greater fascination for her when she vividly recalled the lonely wrecks that were being slowly demolished by pitiless wind and wave and weather near the cockle beds she had visited during those memorable summer holidays.

There were days when she lay for hours in the shelter and shade of the old groynes on the dry sand, never wearying of the sand and sea and sky, but in a half-dreaming, half-waking thoughtfulness, realising that life was good.

Other days when she energetically collected more shells, white stones and seaweed, or caught shrimps and prawns and gathered winkles which she found in profusion in the seaweed on the rocks near the cliffs.

Another day that would long cling to her memory was the day they followed the receding tide under the cliffs and walked for miles along the huge boulders – worn to varying degrees of smoothness by the action of the waves – that had fallen from the towering cliffs above, until they came to the big roadway that led out into the waters of the bay, and picked up winkles and whelks and caught shrimps on the very Sarn itself, and then returned home in order to get past the big cliff head that hid the village from them before the tide came up again.

Coming in sight of the village around the cliff, they encountered a fisherman with a big prawn net, very much bigger than the diminutive shrimping net Mary Eleanor carried, and after a short conversation, he opened a creel he carried slung over his shoulder, and showed them three or four large crabs he had caught.

Mary Eleanor's eyes opened wide at the sight of them and she said she would not like to have one of them catch her toe when paddling in the pools; they must be giant crabs as the prawns were giant shrimps, for she had been playing with little crabs in the seaweed, and they were scarcely bigger than spiders. She remarked they were so funny looking when they ran away because they had to go sideways!

The fisherman promised to send a couple of crabs down to their house the next day, and her aunt having paid him for them, they proceeded home, Mary Eleanor confessing that the ups and downs of the walk had quite tired her out, but had also made her hungry enough to eat a big meal!

All too quickly sped the days of that summer by the seaside, with its many joys of bathing, paddling, shrimping, and playing, and Mary Eleanor was not eager to return to school duties and lessons, for the fascination of outdoor life held her in its grip; she felt that she had learned much during those holiday weeks.

But the exceptionally fine August slipped into September and the equinoctial gales made the beach a less desirable playground, and when the week before school commenced its winter session, a small gale washed away, during a high tide, many of her treasured stones and shells, she was content once more to turn her thoughts toward her lessons and school.

CHAPTER 5

MARY ELEANOR AT THE MISSIONARY MEETING

Ever since Mary Eleanor had come across the big ocean, and had settled in the 'Land of Song' with her relatives, it had been their plain duty to see that she accompanied them to all the services held in the village chapel which they attended; she could not recall having missed one such service during the eleven months which had passed since her advent to the place.

The only child in the household, and not being thought equal to understanding the general conversation as she had not yet acquired the language, it was natural that she was seldom considered when neighbours dropped in, and village gossip was indulged in. The local habit of Anglicising many words of common usage, the introduction of names and places in the talk, in conjunction with gestures of various kinds, made it possible for Mary Eleanor to glean at least the drift of the conversation, and at times, gain quite an insight into matters which were not for her ears.

She had learned from experience not to refer to any of these topics, as reproval was generally sharp. These things were stored up for future reference, and the sum total of the knowledge she had so acquired would have appalled anyone interested in the wholesome training of such a young girl.

She kept a pure mind, and her young character remained uncorrupted with a peculiar reasoning of her own, she withheld from her schoolmates any fact thus brought to her knowledge. It was well for her that she was imbued with such a complete sense of right and wrong; beyond the fact that she was much too young to have acquired an insight into some of the matters discussed in her hearing, no harm seemed done.

It was thus quite in the ordinary course of events that she should hear a great deal concerning the forthcoming mission week, and as this was a topic she instinctively felt could be referred to and enquired about without blame, she had asked many questions of those who knew, and found also to her great delight that she was growing better able to follow the trend of any conversation as new words were constantly being added to her increasing vocabulary of Welsh.

Mary Eleanor possessed, to a remarkable degree, the peculiar faculty which made her, for the time any matter interested her, very thoroughly adopt any ways or feelings pertaining to the subject, as a great dramatic artist might appear to lose identity in personification of a character chosen for presentation. The effect of the present influences was to make her at heart very much a missionary.

Consequently, it was no task to attend the nightly services that might otherwise have been very tedious and trying to the child. Her interest held throughout the week, although she realised her limitations and knew it must be years and years before she could do anything worthwhile towards attaining her present ambition. In the meantime, she would do all she could by absorbing available information on the subject.

Mary Eleanor's ideas on matters of religion were at times decidedly quaint, and the conclusions she invariably arrived at, even after the perusal of such books and articles as would have shaken the faith of many a confirmed and devout Christian by the seemingly incontrovertible arguments contained therein, were such that she never hesitated to talk to God about, because, she said, He always understood the big dictionary words for her, and she always felt sorry for those who wanted to worship something and did not know, just as she did, that God was always in the something that they worshipped, so no matter what they worshipped, it was really God all the time.

Someday, God would make arrangements for them to understand better. She always excused the heathen, and any form of idolatry practised by them, by saying that God would not blame them altogether, only a little, and He would take their sincere worship in their particular form of idolatry as partly His, and so forgive them much because of their sincerity and fidelity, although it would not be towards Him.

She did wish, however, that the fervour expressed in the local missionary meetings might be capable of a more direct application to the cause of the heathen. It seemed such a huge waste of energy when some of the local brethren overflowed in exuberance, and used extravagant expressions in their prayers, an exuberance which seemed to need a further outlet necessitating a more or less heavy thumping of the fist on desk or pew.

'If only he would push a spade into the garden as hard as he knocks the pew, I should think he could grow a great lot of vegetables that he might sell for missionary purposes, and there would not be so much call for "monumentary assistance". I'm not quite sure whether that is the right word or not, but I'm sure almost anyone could work a bit harder and earn a bit more money if they did not get so worn out and waste their strength in thumping the benches. It can't be good for the benches, either, and by the time we can afford to get some natives over here to teach them things, we shall not have a very tidy house of God to show them if they keep on thumping so hard.'

Then, applying the principle to herself, she carefully and secretively took out her diminutive handkerchief and polished the front part of the pew over which she bent her head, with the reflection that it was her duty to set an example to others by keeping her part of God's house in order, and being like a little candle shining in her small corner.

Her active brain could not rest for an instant as she settled herself more comfortably on the faded pew cushion, while the earnest long-winded supplicant sobbingly concluded his prayer amid a chorus of brotherly Amens of varying degrees of heartiness.

It was typical of Mary Eleanor that whenever she found occasion to find fault in others from her point of view, or God's – and she frequently imagined that she could quite understand God's way of looking at an action, whether it were of thought or deed – that she should apply the test to herself, becoming as it were, both accused and accuser, when fault, of greater or less magnitude, appeared to take form in her imaginative noddle.

She even went to the length of inflicting penance on herself for misdeeds or unkind thoughts, if self-detected and time was given for reflection; and who shall say that the habit of judging herself by the standard of right to which she thought others should attain was not instrumental, in a high degree, of forming the child's unusual character?

As the main topic of conversation in the village during the missionary week was of mission affairs in general or any matter pertaining to the holding of the special meetings which would culminate in the Big Meeting (Cwrdd Mawr) on the ensuing Sabbath, Mary Eleanor had gleaned a vast amount of information about the subject, and had imbibed much enthusiasm for the heathen who lived in those far-off lands where the missionaries were sent by the aid of the money collected at these meetings.

This was the third evening of the series, and as she bowed her head reverently when the first participant in the evening's service commenced his prayer, she asked God to keep her from dwelling on the various peculiarities of each in succession. She often wondered why she always felt more wicked when in God's house than when on the beach or by the river, and asked herself why the old man in the corner pew always presented to her such a comical aspect when he was considered a particularly saintly man by her elders.

It was a matter of constant fascination to her to watch him rise to join in the hearty singing of the congregation, and note the usual order of emotions which took possession of him as he sang in quavering tones without the aid of the book, verse after verse of the familiar hymns appropriate to the occasion.

Gripping the edge of the pew, in the second verse, he seemed to lose himself in an ecstasy of feeling that expressed itself in a gentle swaying of the body, occasionally accompanied with extra emphasis of movement that caused his long beard to make a sudden jerky toss upward, for which Mary Eleanor always watched.

If, by any chance, the congregation, carried away by fervour of feeling, repeated the singing of any one verse, the very interesting spectacle of seeing him close his eyes tightly as if to shut out all distracting things from view in order to concentrate on the things of which he sang, kept Mary Eleanor entranced to such a degree that she almost forgot to sit down with the rest of the congregation.

Although the next member of the congregation called upon to take part in the service was one whose performance she always watched with particular interest, she felt constrained to ask God to forgive her because the old man's singing made her think of a circus and clowns, and made her want to laugh, which she knew would be irreverent, and not in keeping with the time and place.

She resolved that when the next hymn was sung, she would look at the other side of the chapel, and not watch the jerks of that beard, however irresistible, and no matter how she might be tempted to look.

Having done her best, as she thought, to absolve herself and clear her besmirched conscience with free confession followed by resolute determination to turn from her wicked ways and follow the path of rectitude, she endeavoured earnestly to concentrate on the prayer that followed the singing of the hymn. She felt certain that there could be no question of sinning if occasionally her mind wandered since she had no means of fully understanding the long Welsh words.

The rhythmic rise and fall of the suppliant's voice as he worked himself up to the usual pitch of fervour, which called for encouraging accompanying ejaculations of praise and agreement, made Mary Eleanor wonder whether the introduction of a similar tone added to her simple evening prayer would increase its efficacy, but decided that it was scarcely suitable for a child. She considered that she ought to arrive at years of discretion before she attempted this addition to her orisons, and anyway, God had always looked after her well enough, even if she did not always get all she wanted of nice things to wear and eat.

She occasionally caught amid the – to her – unintelligible jargon, a word or two of which she had learned the sense, and had placed in the back of her mind to add to the sum total that would someday render her bilingual.

She had recently had many ambitious dreams of being able to use, perhaps, some of the newly acquired words of this difficult language to good purpose, if she ever went to 'Afric's golden sands', or the places inhabited by the poor ignorant heathen; for the nonce, it would seem that her whole being had been filled with this one idea of doing her level best to carry the gospel news to all parts of the world.

The only path that seemed to lead in that direction, was the simple present duty of trying to learn a new language, that she might grow a little wiser on missionary items by listening to and understanding the present week's service better. It was a case of accepting the duty that was nighest and she fervently wished it would not appear quite so much out of place if she brought along a dictionary with her hymn book.

Public opinion, on second thoughts, would have made the dictionary assume huge proportions and prominence, she reflected, so she would have to rely on her memory for some of the words which seemed to take her fancy, and ask their meaning after the service was over.

She sighed as she realised that she could not carry in mind more than four words without getting them hopelessly mixed up, and even as she mentally rehearsed them, she was not sure whether the prefixes had not been slightly jumbled.

Recalling her wandering thoughts to the present with an effort, it dawned on her that the climax of the worthy brother's prayer had been reached, and that it needed but the repetition of a few more sentences of a set form, of which she almost knew the sequence, which he always used to draw together the threads of his various pleadings to close his solicitations.

She prided herself on the fact that she could nearly repeat perfectly this part – ere long she would be able to ask the meaning of the complete ending.

Mentally following these sentences, and forming the words as approximately as she could with silently moving lips, in order to assist her memory by parrot-like repetition of the sounds, she followed the prayer to its conclusion feeling that she had accomplished diligently and without a great deal of deviation from the right, the prayer just offered.

Amid varying adjustments of dolman and cloak, and the general rustle consequent on the changing of posture of the congregation bowed in prayer to a sitting attitude, Mary Eleanor, acting in unison with the rest of the people, reached for her hymn book, at the same time clearing her little throat in readiness for the next hymn, the announcement of which she awaited with close attention.

She had memorised the pronunciation of the words necessary to count up to at least one hundred in this new language, but it puzzled her sorely to know why different persons called the same numbers by different names. For instance, why should eighty be called by some eight tens and by others four twenties? And it certainly meant that she had not only to translate the various words but actually work

out an example in addition such as four and ten
and four twenties for ninety-four.

At times, she almost despaired of ever
knowing exactly when to make use of the names
of all the different figures correctly. She had
only recently grasped the fact that if one were
counting a group of girls, one would not use the
same words as one would for a group of boys,
and she was astonished at the way quite young
children could find the right words to use in
this very difficult language – why, even little
children of five or six could converse readily in
Welsh.

Fortunately for her peace of mind this time,
however, the number given was simple, and she
turned over the leaves of her little black hymn
book, quickly finding the hymn chosen, and
followed the sound of the reading of the words.
She had come across a literal translation of this
verse in a tiny Welsh magazine called *Winllan y
Plant* some time before this and had committed
it to memory. Whenever this hymn was
announced, she sang it mentally in English and
felt that she really was joining in the service;
God knew that she could not always join in,
because it was mostly unintelligible to her,
consequently He frequently had to forgive her
wandering thoughts; of course, He was quite
ready to do that as she had not yet learned
Welsh.

'In the deep and mighty waters
There is none to hold my head
But my only Saviour Jesus
Who was offered in my stead.
He's a Friend in Death's deep river

Mary Eleanor

Holding up my feeble head
With His smile I'll go rejoicing
Through the regions of the dead.'

The third and last of those taking part in the evening's prayers was a white-headed old man who commenced in quiet measured tones his simple address to God, and although he had not announced a hymn in keeping with the all-absorbing topic – missions – his frequent mention of 'the black negro' (y negro du), and 'dying in his sins' (marw yn ei phechodau), convinced Mary Eleanor that he had remembered what he should pray for, even if he had made a mistake in giving out a hymn having no bearing on the subject, and she decided that he must be making use of the right phrases, for the usual undertones of Amens were quite plentiful.

She wondered if God would mind if she did not try to remember any more words, as she felt so very sleepy. It was so warm and the air was not so fresh as out on the beach and anyway she had been very busy in her spare time that day collecting some pretty shells and seaweed, and had gone a long way for some she had seen near one of the old groynes, and somehow her eyelids felt very stiff.

It was quite easy to keep them shut in prayer, as she didn't feel in the least tempted to open them and ... and ... and Mary Eleanor, lulled by the monotone, and wearied by the exertions of her little brain, soon yielded to the many soporific influences, and actually slept as she leaned on her little hands on the front of the pitch-pine pew.

Her body, relaxing as she lost all consciousness in sleep, no longer adequately supported her in her devout posture, and her head becoming heavy in consequence, dropped onto the hymn book shelf sufficiently hard to arouse her. She awoke with a start, looking swiftly yet carefully around to see whether anyone had noticed her lapse.

She glanced in particular at the occupants of the pew in front. She would not have had them know that she had actually been asleep even if it had been only for an instant, as it were. The little girl in front, however, was still turning over the leaves of her hymn book, a habit of hers when she had grown tired of a service, and the boy had still got his head in proper position on his hands.

Still, she almost fancied his eyes were open, and that he could see her with a sidewise glance, and had probably noticed that she had been asleep.

Comforting herself with the assurance that he never teased her, no matter what happened, although she knew from experience that he always seemed to know all about her, she tried to keep awake and in a proper attitude.

Fortunately, the last prayer was soon finished, and with the singing of a final verse or two, the service ended, much to her relief, as she was sure that she could not have kept awake for another prayer.

As she left the pew with the others for the aisle, she caught for a very fleeting second an amused indulgent twinkle in the eyes of the boy as he joined the crowd in the aisle.

The usual exchange of conversation that always followed the services as the congregation emerged from the chapel was soon over and Mary Eleanor, too tired to recall any new words, was glad to get home and go to bed.

It did not take her long to disrobe, and as she knelt to say her prayers in a less devout manner than was her usual wont, she felt sure that God, perhaps, got a little bit tired sometimes, and would not mind if her talk to Him was very short that night. Certain set verses and forms she went through, beginning with 'Jesus, tender Shepherd, hear me,' scarcely sensing any of the words, and with a child's supreme trust, she concluded her devotions by adding, 'Dear God, I'm too tired to look after any more negroes. I leave them to You.'

Creeping into her little bed, she was soon lost in deep slumber, having left in the hands of a Higher Power without the slightest misgiving, the many duties she felt too tired and sleepy to continue.

Would that we might emulate her simple faith and trust, when the more serious problems of life give us cause for anxious thought and worry!

CHAPTER 6

MARY ELEANOR'S FIRST
HERRING SEASON

Summer was a thing of the past. The annual five weeks of holidaymaking was long since over, and the daily routine of schoolwork had settled down to its wonted regularity, when Mary Eleanor noticed one morning the big brown fishing nets spread out in the backyard as she cleaned her boots prior to going to school.

The mornings were by no means so warm as they had been, and she hastened over her task in the chill wind that seemed to nip her fingers and make them slow to obey her will. She had seen the nets spread out on the pebbly beach during the summer and had been very curious about the big pieces of cork attached to them, and had seen one of the fishermen mending them in readiness for the winter's herring fishing when they received their yearly overhauling.

As she noticed the great nets laid out, she gathered that the boat that used these nets each year was soon to go out for its share of the haul of herrings that served the villagers as a staple article of diet during the winter.

She found also that the principal topic of talk in school hours was an interesting discussion about the number of boats in readiness for the season, and which boat would carry the largest number of nets, and sometimes one of the older boys would probably announce the fact that he was going to be out with one of the boats one night. This statement generally elicited a chorus of similar claims until all of the biggest lads were found likely to be absent on certain days in consequence of being out on the waters of the bay all night with the herring fishing.

The herring boats seemed so very small to hold so many nets and fish, Mary Eleanor thought, and she was pleased when she found that the men of the village could undertake the arduous task of the fishing without the aid of the women. She had seen the women perform so many heavy duties in the village that she wondered if she would ever be able to take her share in the village labours. Why, even her aunt and those she thought never likely to do any manual labour had been fully occupied in the potato fields recently, digging up the crop of potatoes on the interminable rows and leaving them to dry off as they worked steadily to the end of the rows before picking them up.

At intervals along the row there were big sacks to hold the potatoes, which were sorted into three sizes – seed, eating and pig potatoes – during the picking-up process.

Mary Eleanor had been absent from school one day in order that she might go with her relatives to the distant potato field on the hill near the village. The long hill climb to the farm where two long rows of the field of potatoes belonged to them for a small rental wearied Mary Eleanor too much to make her eager to try her hand at the digging, and she was given the privilege of having a rest on the bundle of sacks before she gave her small quota of help in the picking up.

After a rest, during which Mary Eleanor had been impressed with a sense of great quiet and peace, she rambled along the hedge in search of blackberries, although it was late in the season, but found so few that she concluded that her mouth was the best place for them, and wished with all her heart that it was time to open the big basket of food which had been so laboriously carried up the long hill for their use when the dinner hour arrived.

She was relieved when she was told that it was time to go to the farm to fetch a bottle of buttermilk as the beverage to accompany the luncheon wrapped in the basket.

The rows of potatoes had been marked out according to the number of rows rented by a family, and she rejoiced that only two instead of eight or ten were needed in her family, and if the weather kept fine that day she knew their rows would be finished, the potatoes picked up and bagged ready to be brought down by the farmer's cart in a day or two.

When Mary Eleanor got back into the field with the buttermilk she found that the two rows were at least half dug, and the potatoes were drying on the top of the soil, and they would be ready for collecting into the bags very shortly.

The climb up the hill had made her very hungry and the frugal meal was thoroughly enjoyed in consequence. They were up quite high above the sea, and Mary Eleanor spent some time in gazing 'all around the edge of the world' as she described it to her elders. As the day was clear, the distant hills to the north side of the bay stood out in full majesty against the clear sky. The Snowdon range in the far distance with the nearer view of Cader Idris and the many hills beyond the Dovey Estuary loomed up in great grandeur, and she wished she knew the names of them all as they were silhouetted against that blue sky.

Swinging around to the east and south, the big Plynlymon range dominated the horizon and held her attention for a while. It was with a huge sigh that she completed the circle of her survey as she turned to the west and looked out over the waters of the bay.

'What makes you sigh like that, Mary Eleanor?' queried her aunt.

'I always thought it would be very nice to climb up to the top of a mountain, but we are only on the top of a little hill and it made me rather tired to come here this morning, so I am afraid that it would be very hard to climb a mountain unless I can become a better walker as I grow older,' she replied.

'Well, as the mountains are too far away today, it is no good thinking about them, or worrying your head about impossible things. Wait until you grow up.'

'I'm not worrying, only wondering. Sometimes I feel I'd like to be like a seagull able to go just wherever I want to go, without any trouble, just glide along so easily, float on the sea or fly swiftly up and along the river as those birds are doing over the Dovey,' Mary Eleanor answered, waving her arms about in fancied imitation of a sea bird's flight.

'Even the seagulls have to get their daily food,

Mary Eleanor,' was the quiet reminder, which brought her wandering thoughts back to the potato field and its present urgent call for a little help even from her childish hands.

'Supposing you fill the bucket with the small potatoes and I'll empty it into the bag when it is full,' her aunt continued.

At once Mary Eleanor willingly undertook the task, listening the meanwhile to the conversation carried on between her aunt and helper, and she gathered from the few Welsh words she had learned that the potato crop was proving a good one that year and that if the herring season shortly to arrive proved successful, the villagers would be unusually well provided for during the coming winter.

There were various surmises about the 'family' pigs in the village. Some were very shortly to meet their fate; others would not be ready for killing until near Christmas.

The porcine population was another generally unfailing source of food among the fisherfolk, and Mary Eleanor had many a time partaken of the savoury dish they called 'stiw cig moch' (pork stew). To be made in perfection this required long slow cooking in the big stewpot hooked onto the chain in the wide chimney over the peat fire, with a final rich crisp browning of the big potatoes and succulent spare rib by piling onto the lid of the stewpot red-hot chunks of peat.

Mary Eleanor liked this satisfying tasty dish immensely and was always sorry when it could no longer be eked out for another meal by adding a little water and finely chopped onion and a pinch of salt and then warmed up again.

It was quite likely, she gathered from the conversation, that a near neighbour contemplated having her pig killed during the coming week, and since the kitchen refuse of Mary Eleanor's home had been religiously saved and given to this neighbour to help her in the rearing thereof, the usual return in the shape of a bit of spare rib was consequently expected.

Thus occupied in mind and hand, Mary Eleanor's afternoon in the potato field passed swiftly away, and when she had trudged down the long hill to the village with her elders, she had been so sleepy and tired that bedtime came none too soon; it was beyond her power to keep awake when she knelt to her prayers by her bedside.

Her aunt, following her up soon afterwards in order to see that the candle was safely put out, found her fast asleep in a half-kneeling, half-reclining posture against the bed, and lifted the heavily sleeping child onto the bed.

The potato harvesting was now over throughout the village, and the possible heavy herring catch was the hourly topic of discussion among young and old, male and female.

All of this was new to Mary Eleanor, and she listened attentively to any conversation on the subject. Sensitive to a degree about knowing a thing or the reason why certain tasks were undertaken, she often accumulated useful knowledge through sheer fear of being ignorant on any matter when questioned, and having, in consequence, to endure ridicule.

She was heavily handicapped in her self-imposed task because so many of the Welsh words and expressions seemed beyond her, and she found that the Welsh of her Bible was very different from the language as currently spoken in the village.

She despaired of ever knowing when to use the correct Welsh words for a reply in the affirmative or negative, and the many idioms used, together with different forms of spelling a word simply and solely because of the gender used at the time, were ever a great hindrance to her rapid acquisition of the language.

The absence of the neuter gender in the language was but another complexity. There seemed no sense in calling an article 'he' or 'she'. It sounded so utterly ridiculous in English, and she never seemed able to reason why some things were considered of sufficient masculinity or femininity to warrant their being so designated.

She could understand why the sun and moon might be 'he' or 'she', for in English they sometimes called the sun 'Old Sol', and that could only mean a 'he', while the use of the pretty name 'Fair Luna' in reference to the moon at once put it in the feminine class; where the kettle, fender, coal box, and every known article obtained their various masculine or feminine attributes and qualities was a bewildering problem beyond her ingenuity.

After a few days of fine settled weather she was told that the boat having the nets belonging to their place had gone out with the others and that there was promise of a good haul of herrings. This proved to be the case, and Mary

Eleanor found on coming home from school that large numbers of herrings had been carried home and placed in all sorts of receptacles.

As the women folk were too much occupied to attend to her, she was told to get her own tea and be on hand to run errands or help in her small way. The novelty of seeing so many fish and wondering what was to become of them made her hasten her meal to witness the proceedings.

Large wooden tubs, which had been scrupulously scrubbed and soaked during the week in anticipation of a herring glut, were in readiness together with some large loaves of salt. A thick layer of salt had been strewn on the bottom of each tub, and as the fish were gutted and cleaned they were tightly packed in neat layers in the tubs, alternating with layers of salt, until the tubs were full, and the final layer of salt laid on thick enough to cover the fish from sight.

At least two tubs full of fish were packed and salted that night, and Mary Eleanor had listened to the account of the previous night's heavy run of herrings, which had filled the nets of the boats to breaking point in some cases, and heard how some of the nets had been too old and ought never to have been used when the weather conditions favoured such a great run of herrings.

It was late when operations were over and Mary Eleanor had long held the lantern to assist in the safe packing of their winter supply of fish. She had made the womenfolk laugh when she enquired if it was usual to eat so much salt with fish that had come from salt water; she thought it quite possible that sea fish would keep much better than fresh-water fish because they had always been in salt water!

The next morning, being a Saturday, held a treat for the child when she was told to go to the beach to watch one of the herring boats come ashore. Clambering down over the big sea fence, she ran quickly over the firm sand to where a group of schoolchildren and women awaited the receding of the tide from around one of the biggest herring boats, which already almost rested on the sandy beach, its nets and the glistening shining fish ready for distribution into baskets, buckets, sacks, and pans immediately the receding sea permitted.

Thrown to one end of the boat were seven or eight large skates (morgathod), and she overheard the remark that these had been numerous in the shoal of herrings during the night; they were a fish enjoyed the inhabitants but their presence was not much relished by the herring-fishers, as torn nets and consequent escape of many herrings was the result, and when the weather proved propitious, little time could be given to mending of nets. There had also been a number of porpoises (pysgodyn du) in the bay, and they had played havoc with the nets.

Leaping into the water the boatmen laid sturdy hands on either side of the boat and with a strong shove or two in efforts well-timed with the waves' assistance, forced the boat almost high and dry, so that little time elapsed ere the fish were being thrown into the various articles on hand to receive them, being divided according to the number of nets in the boat, extra shares being given to the men who had worked in the boat all night, and an especial share being allotted to the boat (siar y cwch).

Rhythmically and regularly they were gleaned from the enmeshing nets, and the query 'Whose share is this?' put to a member of the crew, who, for equity's sake, turned his back to the division of the catch and gave a reply, quickly acted upon, as each 'bwrw' or 'throw' was allocated.

It did not take long ere the boat was cleared of its silvery scaly burden and the several skates with the few whiting which had been trapped with the herrings in the nets were divided. These whiting were not held in much esteem at this time by the villagers, but Mary Eleanor was very fond of them as prepared at her home, and when told by a friendly fisherman to run home for a bucket so that she could have some of them, made off excitedly for the bucket and thanked the donor so nicely when receiving the whiting that he was impelled to say, 'Tell your aunt to send up by and by; she can have one of the skates to cook for you.'

Mary Eleanor fared sumptuously on fish during the ensuing fortnight, herring especially, which was dished up in many forms, fried and baked and pickled. The glut of the herring harvest proclaimed itself to the nostrils by savoury smells from one end of the village to the other. My Lord Herring was ubiquitous, and the supply of fish for rich and poor throughout the village was assured – even the poorer folk, owning neither nets nor boats, being able to purchase a few 'hundreds' (six score and an extra 'throw') to salt down for a reserve store, as the heavy hauls each night so cheapened the fish that it became scarcely worthwhile putting out from land for more.

Later on in the winter, Mary Eleanor found that at stated periods a couple of dozen of the much-salted fish were taken from the tubs and washed and soaked in fresh water until they were considered fairly free from the preserving salt and wiped dry and threaded onto a long stick or thick wire poked through their gills. This was then hung up to dry somewhere under the eaves out of the reach of possible marauding cats. When a 'stenin' (a local corruption of 'ysgadenyn' – a herring) as they were called, was wanted for a supper relish, or even perhaps the noonday meal, combined with a saucepan full of great mealy potatoes boiled in their jackets and just bursting in floury whiteness, the number of herrings required was taken from the stick and cooked on a toaster over the glowing red-hot embers of coal or peat fires, and the meal was one not to be despised, especially when approached with the hearty appetite of a rapidly growing child.

The flavour of the 'stenin' was enhanced, in Mary Eleanor's opinion, by being served on one of the many picture plates from the old Welsh dresser, the ones most frequently in use for her supper depicting scenes which the potter's mind conceived to be illustrative of the Ten Commandments – Cain in the act of slaying Abel, with the words of the sixth commandment in plain print beneath the gaudily coloured picture, or the fourth commandment plate with a group of four people attired in garments of early Victorian style, or earlier, the lady with her crinoline skirt and gay shawl accompanying her husband and children to church.

The potter's art in printing and painting scenes was a source of unfailing entertainment to Mary Eleanor, and when in the spring the big and little jugs were taken down from their queer old hooks for a more thorough cleaning than the daily dusting afforded, she was delighted by being permitted to read the quaint mottoes and verses on some of them.

One side of one of the white jugs was covered with an intertwining, unending device on which ran the words:

'Love is a virtue that endures forever
A link of matchless jewels none can sever.
They on Whose Breast this Sacred Love doth place.
Shall after Death the fruits thereof embrace.
Among the many pleasures that we prove
None are so real as the joys of Love.
For true Love is worth commending,
Still beginning, never ending.'

The reverse side of this quaint jug had a series of mottoes, encircled with a marvellous wreath of flowers of gay and varied hues.

'Do well and have well.
Have God and have all.
Do right, and fear no shame.
God will help, none can hinder.
Providence is better than riches.'

Another jug which claimed much of her

attention had a picture of a 'Club Day' and beneath the picture was this verse:

'To explain my good Friends our first and best aim
Is to succour the sick feed the Old help the lame
In a Cause such as this E'en the Poorest would pay
And work hard to provide against such a Club Day.'

On turning this jug over, she read:

'We are Good Fellows
When we act and
Do the thing which is Right.'

This centre motto was surrounded by a scroll in which the following couplet was placed:

'How grand in Age, How fair in Youth, is Holy Friendship, Love and Truth.'

She laughed at the funny way the artist had chosen to place the capital letters and she thought the flowers were very unusual. She had to be very careful in handling the jugs, as they were very old and consequently of great value, and she felt that she had been accorded special favour when allowed to hold them and read their old-fashioned verses and maxims.

She liked best of all the jug with the double true lover's knot, 'still beginning, never ending.' Many a time during that winter did she think over the queer lettering on some of the jugs, and she always loved to watch the fitful light from the peat fire playing on the old copper lustre jugs which alternated with the lighter jugs with the interesting mottoes, and felt honoured when her supper was served on a commandment plate, or her bread and milk in a fancifully coloured basin which belonged to the dresser, and generally reposed by an immense Swansea basin enriched by roses and foliage of crude design but withal very quaint.

The old Welsh dresser seemed to be very crowded with its plenitude of jugs, and owing to its completeness was held to be a very fine example of its kind and equalled the old Grandfather clock near it in antiquity and richness of hue of age-toned oak. Just inside of the lower door of the clock, where one gained access to weights when necessary to wind or regulate it, were chalk marks by which tally was kept of such transactions as the number of nets lent to a boat or similar affairs of which it was deemed essential that a record should be kept.

Mary Eleanor was frequently amused at the primitive method used, but was often privileged during that winter to see the clock door consulted in order to settle minor disputes and felt that she must admit it was a very effective way of keeping tally, for no one questioned the accuracy of the chalk marks in the old clock when once placed there, generally with a witness to ensure the absolute justness of the chalked-up entry.

CHAPTER 7

MARY ELEANOR LEARNS NEW GAMES AND CUSTOMS

The herring season well over, the excitement that kept the schoolchildren constantly surmising which boat would catch the largest number of fish abated, and beyond an occasional reference to the biggest boat as having caught the largest number of herrings in recent years during one of the best fishing nights of the season, and having created a record in quantity of 'hundreds', the topic was dropped at school.

Each day in school brought its novelties to Mary Eleanor. In the arithmetic lessons came those funny pounds, shillings, and pence, so markedly different to compute compared with the American dollars and cents – for examples in arithmetic where dollars and cents were used were so very much easier – but priding herself on being quick at figures, Mary Eleanor applied herself diligently to the new coinage she had to learn.

She had many a laugh over her difficulty in remembering the names of the different coins, and how many of them made up a sovereign. Florins and half-crowns, groats and threepenny bits were her stumbling blocks; one day, having read a story about a 'nimble ninepence', she convulsed her teacher by stating that it must be an obsolete coin, as she had been enquiring about one for over a month, and no one seemed to know anything about it.

Mary Eleanor

She found no difficulty in her English lessons, which were simple to her, although so very hard for her fellow schoolmates. She reasoned that it would have been very much harder for her to write or read in Welsh, and that it was no laughing matter when they made what appeared to her to be absurd mistakes, and bit her lips hard to prevent a suspicion of a smile escaping her.

In spelling also she easily led her class, but the whole class and the teacher were one day astonished when Mary Eleanor spelled out the word 'seize' after two or three had failed to place the 'e' and 'i' in the correct order. In American fashion, Mary Eleanor's pronunciation of the 'z' sounded 'zee', and it was thought that she had used a 'c'.

Colouring vividly at the misunderstanding, she courageously, although inwardly trembling, said she had spelled it correctly.

'But you said "c"!' came a chorus of voices.

'No, I said "zee", the last letter in the alphabet,' Mary Eleanor stoutly asserted.

'That is "zed"!' laughed the class.

'We used to call it "izzard" sometimes in school, but in spelling a word we always said "zee",' explained Mary Eleanor when the laughter had subsided.

The teacher, having told the class that all countries did not sound letters alike, and that Mary Eleanor would have written the word correctly, changed the occupation of the class from spelling to reading, Mary Eleanor privately resolving that she would call the letter 'zed' in school and 'zee' in her self-communings at

85

home.

She desired to be 'friends' with all her schoolfellows and disliked anything that led to a scene, or brought her into the foreground. Because it had fallen to her lot to be an American girl among Welsh girls who barely spoke English, she sensed an undercurrent of jealousy when her knowledge of English proved a cause of superiority in her class.

She tried to avoid any seeming triumph and many a battle royal did she have with her conscience over the question. Would it be acting a lie to spell a word incorrectly when she knew the right way, if by so doing so she gave another girl a chance sometimes to get ahead of her, was a frequently debated matter, and the ever-recurring question that has made many an older and wiser person pause, 'Is it right to do wrong that good may result?' never would solve itself when she took herself to task about it.

She was initiated by the girls into a number of new games and of them all, the most fascinating, principally because she never attained great proficiency in it, was the game of 'knucklebones', or as the girls pronounced it 'nicktons'. This game was played with four well-polished knucklebones perseveringly saved from the legs of mutton purchased for a weekend whenever the pecuniary resources of the family permitted such a luxury, and a marble.

While the marble bounced up from the stone step on which the game was played, the girl players deftly picked up one, two, three or four of the 'nicktons' at a time, keeping the marble regularly on the bounce. The game was quite complicated, as the girls rang the changes in the order of picking up and counting, and it required a good deal of dexterity especially when the bones scattered themselves rather far apart when thrown from the hand in time to catch the marble.

During the noon hour and 'playtime' the school steps were fully occupied by the older girls playing the game.

There was an interesting variety of hopscotch which was played by some of the girls and which they called 'Ecsil'. The nearest word that Mary Eleanor could find to interpret their name for this game was Exile. She was very fond of the game as it could be played by a varying number from two to six.

Picking up one of the small flat stones of which there were plenty by the roadside and choosing a clear level space of ground, a square, subdivided into nine other squares, was marked out on the ground in varying degrees of exactitude, plus an extra square at the top right-hand corner.

The stone, having been thrown very carefully into the first space by the player standing in the extra square, was gently propelled into the second space by the right foot, hopping fashion (one lost one's turn it, for any reason, the left foot touched the ground, or the stone ever so slightly rested on one of the marking-out lines). The fourth space in order of play was a resting

3	2	1	Home
4	9	8	
5	6	7	

space, and it was permitted to stand on both feet before proceeding around the outer square to the next resting space (9).

From nine to two and thence home, without a mishap, or first home in spite of mistakes, constituted the game.

Some girls were quite adroit in hopping after the stone and by gentle coaxing when not carefully watched, could work the stone slightly back if trespassing on a line. If caught, there followed great accusations of 'Cafflo, cafflo,' (Cheat, cheat,) with denials of more or less vigour.

She was as great an enthusiast as any of the girls at the game, until one day, when playing with a little girl friend near her home, one of the village 'ancients', a deacon in one of the village chapels, took them seriously to task for being so wicked as to play a game attended by such ruinous results to their boots.

As his words were cutting and caustic and made them both feel uncomfortable, they left the game unfinished, and their monitor still reproving their many peccadilloes. He had enlarged on their probable participation in many games that were destructive to clothes, and held them responsible for influencing poorer children to play the game whose parents could ill afford the money to buy them footwear.

Mary Eleanor always played Ecsil in the school grounds or on the beach after this scolding, and avoided the deacon whenever possible, rejoicing in the fact that he did not attend her chapel, as his presence there would have made her feel most uncomfortable on the days she tried to be really good because it was so long and tedious a task to sit for such a long time in the awkward pews when she could not understand a word of the proceedings.

She had many a laugh with her little girl friend over the way they slunk away from this uncalled-for homily. Mary Eleanor reflected that if the game were really so destructive as he made it out to be, she would have been prohibited from playing it long before this from reasons of economy. Consequently, she felt free to indulge in it, in spite of the interfering deacon, because it was known at home that she played it almost daily.

Thinking it over sometimes as she put on her boots in the mornings before school, she wished it would wear out boots a bit faster, for she oftener than not had to wear boots that were too small for her.

Rapidly growing, her foot, of course, kept pace with the rest of her, and it became quite a question to keep her feet comfortable. She found that dosing the boots with olive oil helped them to fit easier, and therefore put it on her boots oftener than she otherwise would have done, since she disliked the job intensely.

It was customary at that time to order 'uppers' from the village cobbler, and he then made the stout school boots after measuring the foot.

At first each pair were comfortable but as the soles wore through, the uppers paid more than one visit to the cobbler ere they were discarded.

Because of their very excellent quality they would not wear out easily, and while the plan was to be commended when one's foot had ceased to grow, yet for the growing foot of a child it was false economy.

Anyway, Mary Eleanor's clothes never seemed to be in just the right stage of 'fitness', some being made too big to meet the exigencies of her case, and others, from motives of economy, having to last as long as it was possible to put them on before they were regarded as useless – she, being the only child in the house, could not hand down to smaller fry clothes not worn out but outgrown.

Skipping ropes were very much in demand when the colder weather came, and the possessor of a good smooth heavy skipping rope was sure of companions enough to do their share in turning the rope while 'cup-saucer' and 'pepper and salt' and all sorts of stunts were done rhythmically in the regularly revolving rope.

The girls had to find a quiet corner for their skipping, for the boys at the same period were either choosing their cherished 'Ecsil' sites for their marble games, or playing a game of 'Bando', a species of hockey, or else whipping their tops in the choicest places and shooting with unerring aim at the old school bell with all sorts and sizes of catapults, and the missiles had to be avoided as they fell to the ground.

A very sharp frost following heavy rains that had flooded the Common gave many an hour's sliding on the ice, and if hobnails were not already in one's boots, parents were importuned to have them put in, as sliding was so very much better with stout hobnails in the boots than without them, and one was more likely to be given a pull on the biggest sheet of ice by one of the boys fortunate enough to possess skates; if one only had leather soles, one proved too heavy a weight – hobnails or steel protectors ensured at least one ride while the ice lasted.

November brought the Hiring Fairs in the nearby town, and Mary Eleanor heard many a tale of fun enjoyed and jokes played, told by the older girls, most of whom went to at least one of the hiring Mondays. They brought home immense sticks of rock and generously shared bits of their 'fairings' with the less fortunate ones.

Mary Eleanor learned that the Hiring Fairs were the three Mondays on which anyone requiring the services of a 'morwyn' (maidservant) or 'gwas' (manservant) made a special journey to the nearby town on those days when lads and lasses of the surrounding hamlets and villages foregathered in order to 'cyflogi' or be bound for a year's service to a master or mistress chosen on one of the days.

If, after a series of questionings and agreements on both sides the contract seemed a suitable one, it became binding when a piece of silver varying from a shilling to half a crown in value (designated an 'ernes' (earnest or pledge of the transaction)), was given by the prospective master or mistress and accepted by the future servant, a farm servant on being bound receiving an earnest of half a crown, plus a whip, presumably symbolistic of his calling.

Occasionally, after accepting the coins and mingling among the crowds in the town, one so bound regretted the bargain, or met with a better 'chance' for the year and wished to break the first agreement, and would hasten to find the other contracting party in order to return the 'ernes'. Then would ensue a hurried search along the streets, and possibly in the railway station at the last minute, to return the coin and cancel the agreement; it usually remained binding, however, if employer and employee at the close of the day had not again exchanged coins.

Sometimes the employed one would endeavour to avoid taking any of the year's wage until the twelve months were up and so received the full wage bargained for on the hiring day at the end of the year's service.

Mary Eleanor heard of one maid from the remote mountainside, who had been bound for the sum of fifteen pounds, refusing to accept two £5 notes and five golden sovereigns in payment, maintaining that she had bargained for the fifteen sovereigns and her parents had warned her against paper money of any description, her mistress consequently having to search the village for change of the £5 notes in order that the full wage might be paid in coin, not paper.

The Hiring Fairs were made the occasion for much merriment, and as the country lads and lasses gathered in the town, their amusement was catered for by the usual crowd of hucksters and small showmen. The shops were laden with all sorts of outfits likely to be requisitioned by purchasers laying in a supply of clothing for use during the year in their new places of employment, and money seemed plentiful, many going to the town in order to join in the fun and merriment and come home laden with 'fairings'.

Mary Eleanor had one of the big sticks of rock given her at home, and the sweet was indulged in by half-inch lengths a few times a day, so that it lasted a whole week, and had to be cleared quickly in the end – a procedure which met Mary Eleanor's full approval – for it grew decidedly stickier, in another sense, each successive day.

Mary Eleanor had always found her schoolmates very generous in sharing whatever fell to their lot, or that they were able to procure, and many a slice of raw swede was consumed by them in school hours, in all stages of cleanliness, as one or other of the children proudly produced a swede filched from a field or farmer's waggon carting swedes.

Unless she had a clean pinafore or handkerchief to wipe off some of the griminess of the swede, Mary Eleanor after thanking the donor put her piece away until able to rinse it under the road pump near the school.

Another great favourite in the edible line in school was 'liquorice ball' or 'niklas ball' as the name was corrupted by the children. This toothsome demulcent made its usual appearance when a snap of cold weather occurred, and coughs and colds were prevalent.

The black sticks were sold either whole or in portions and when quite fresh from the shop and not exposed to the action of the air, it had a brittleness that enabled one to chip off with a smart blow on a knife, small pieces that were just right for sucking in the mouth with comfort.

Great fun was experienced from surreptitious showing of black tongues and teeth when a bigger chip than usual was being sucked and sometimes the explosive laughter of a child overmuch tickled and amused at the sight caused a search by the teacher and consequent confiscation of the primary cause.

The excitement and interest aroused by the Hiring Fairs were not over when the evening singing practices for the Christmas concerts began, and Mary Eleanor's evenings were frequently spent, in company with the children of her chapel, in learning new part songs and anthems for that momentous occasion.

Dialogues and recitations were also tried over at these rehearsals, and the Christmas concert at Mary Eleanor's chapel was always a friendly challenge to another chapel's members who held their annual celebration on New Year's Day.

Great rivalry and emulation existed between the two chapels, each striving to at least equal and if possible excel the other in quality of entertainment.

Christmas trees were not so much in evidence as Mary Eleanor had hoped for; in fact, they proved to be merely the topics of conversation as belonging to the realm of things unattainable in the village.

The Christmas decorations on the stage consisted of well-berried holly and trails of hardy ivy culled from the hedges on the roadside leading to the next village in sufficient quantity to cover the front of the raised platform on which the 'côr mawr' and the 'côr y plant' (the big choir and the children's choir) were placed on Christmas night.

The altos, tenors and basses were transferred from one choir to another, according to the piece rendered – the transference a bit difficult, consequent on having to scale the pulpit at the rear of the platform, or be exposed to the critical gaze of the audience as they crossed over behind the seat of the Chairman of the evening (usually a prominent member of the chapel with a fairly deep pocket – at least, for that night).

It was a night of great excitement and the chapel was always filled to its utmost capacity by proud parents and friends who clapped enthusiastically at the rendering of each item, whether it were recitation, solo, duet, dialogue, or anthem.

Murmurs of approval and congratulations were many as the audience complacently agreed that the occasion was a great improvement on every previous one and the rival chapel of course could not be expected to outdo them on the coming New Year's night.

Christmas week was, as a matter of course, a school holiday, and Mary Eleanor learned that groups of children would be calling around on New Year's Day for 'Clenig', and she learned the refrain, and, with earnest application, the words of a number of the little doggerels sung by the children in varying high-pitched voices, sometimes discordant, harsh and hurried, again very sweetly and shyly rendered, according to the age of the group singing for the 'Clenig' at the door.

The words of the little songs were strange and difficult in Mary Eleanor's mouth, as most strange languages prove even to grown-ups, and she had many a laugh over her awkwardness in controlling her tongue in some of the words and finding out what they all meant.

She was not allowed to go from house to house with any of the children as her aunt said only the poorer ones and those much younger than herself went. She was amused at the little bags of calico with drawstrings some of them carried in which to put the pennies obtained at the doors after their efforts at singing the New Year's greetings – the total finally being divided equally among the group of singers.

The most frequently sung was the following:

'Dydd Calan cynta'r flwyddyn
'Rwy'n dyfod ar eich traws,
I mofyn am y geiniog
Neu glwt o fara 'chaws.
Os nagos genych ceiniog
'Dwi'n mofyn dim ond hedd
Cyn daw Dydd Calan nesaf
Bydd llawer yn y bedd.'

After clearing of throats and a pause for breath, the children generally attacked the next doggerel with more confidence:

'Mi godais yn foreu
Mi gerddais yn ffernig
I dy Mr Jones (or whoever it might be)
I mofyn am lenig.'

If the well-meant efforts of the children and the generosity of those in the house brought results of cake and pence or even a humble slice of bread and butter – all very acceptable to hungry children with appetites whetted by their exertions in the keen morning air – they chimed in broken chorus:

'Blwyddyn Newydd Dda,
Llon'd y ty o dda.'

Failing to elicit a response, which sometimes happened when demands had proved too numerous and importunate, they left shouting loudly,

'Blwyddyn Newydd Drwg,
Llon'd y ty o fwg ...'

... amid as great a clatter as possible.

Sometimes, instead of pence or cake, the children would be given some home-made toffee, or a stick of 'cyflaith' (treacle candy). These were two confections much in evidence at this season of the year, and some of the older girls were quite expert in making them. The butteriness and brittleness of the toffee almost always being commented on, also the pull-ability of the treacle candy sticks, well-buttered hands having 'pulled' the treacle candy until it became almost golden in hue.

The point Mary Eleanor cared most about was the eat-ability of either and only objected to toffee or cyflaith when it had 'caught' on the saucepan and in consequence, tasted burnt.

She was permitted to have a couple of friends one evening to watch the making of toffee at her home and have a pleasant evening. This she greatly enjoyed, and consequently did not envy older girls when they told how they had visited some of the farms at night in company with lads of their age for a night of toffee and cyflaith making and fun, arriving home in the wee small hours of the morning.

Altogether Mary Eleanor decided that although Santa Claus had not paid her a visit that Christmas, and no Christmas trees had been seen, there were compensations, and she supposed different countries always had different customs in almost all things, and someday she would grow quite used to them, and she was content.

CHAPTER 8

MARY ELEANOR LEARNS ABOUT LOCAL SUPERSTITIONS

Linking arms as they emerged from the weekly Band of Hope meeting held at the chapel, Mary Eleanor and a few of her friends went down the street towards their homes. It was an extremely dark night, and they could only find their way along by glimpsing the pale light of a candle or lamp through the blinds of some of the houses.

Suddenly, one of the more timorous of the girls called out, 'Hist! Byddwch ddistaw!' in tones of such half fear and command that they halted.

'Whatever *is* the matter, Jane?' questioned one or two of them.

'Don't you know that there is a "bwbach" (hobgoblin) here nearly every night?' she whispered.

'Oh, dear! Oh, dear!' ejaculated the others, huddling closer to each other.

'I thought I heard something move, and that's why I told you to stop and be quiet,' she continued in a hoarse whisper.

'What is a bwbach, Jane?' Mary Eleanor quietly asked in an awed voice.

'Oh, an awful old thing that comes after you, and frightens you nearly to death!' was the answer.

'Ych a fi!' The girls shuddered. 'Are you sure there is one here, Jane?' they asked.

'Yes, indeed, my brother John told me that he and David were walking along here one night last week when he saw it, and it started to come after them and they ran like mad things and got away from it!' answered Jane. 'Let's wait back there until someone comes along.'

'Go on, you big silly! There is no such thing as a bwbach now. They are afraid to be near houses, anyway, if there are any! I'm not afraid of the old things! Come on, girls, follow me!' said Margaret, one of the group more daring than the others.

With a quick response to the bravado in Margaret's voice, the group of girls made a wild dash past the empty space between two houses where Jane had fancied she had heard an unusual noise, and on reaching the proximity of a lighted window not far from the spot, with one accord stopped to get their breath and look back at the fearsome place.

'Oh, my goodness, we *did* run! My heart is thumping hard! You can almost hear it!' said one of them.

'Mine was thumping hard *before* we started to run. I was afraid to breathe almost, for fear the bwbach would hear me!' gasped Jane.

'I don't think there *are* any of the nasty old things! They only tell you so to frighten you! I will ask Mam when I go home,' said Margaret.

'What made John run away then? I asked David and he said they both ran away as fast as they could from the old thing!' said Jane.

'What shape did they say it was, then, if they saw it?' demanded Margaret.

'They were too frightened to look at it to find out, they said,' answered Jane.

'See! There is someone coming down the road

with a little lantern. If we wait here, we can follow whoever it is until we get home,' said practical Margaret.

The light of the lantern as it grew nearer lit up the road and the girls watched the intervening space grow less with relief.

Then the unexpected happened. Out from the dark space between the two houses slowly ambled a poor old donkey that belonged to a carrier in the village.

With relieved derisive shouts of laughter the girls looked at each other in half ashamed manner, then without waiting for the lantern-bearer, ran down the village street to their respective homes accompanied by a confused jumble of sentences and laughter as they made fun of their own fears, and declared that whenever they heard of another bwbach, it would only be a donkey and no one could possibly be afraid of poor old Neddy!

As Mary Eleanor went into her home, she was asked what made her so excited and warm, and she laughingly recounted how they had been so frightened and that the bwbach had proved to be only old Neddy after all.

'But why was Jane so very frightened when she thought there was a bwbach there?' she asked of her elders. 'Are there such things in this country?'

'Nonsense, child, of course not! Someone has been telling tales and frightening the child and she has believed them,' was the reply that eased any doubt she might have remaining on the subject.

'I should not mind believing in fairies, for

there must be many more good ones than bad ones, I think, but Jane said this old thing came after you and frightened you nearly to death!' remarked Mary Eleanor.

'Oh, they used to say all sorts of rubbish in the village, and Jane has probably been listening to some of the old gossips. There are some of the old folks now who declare they have seen such things but everyone knows better than to credit their fancies about such silly old things,' she was told.

'Come along now, for your supper and then to bed, and don't worry your head any more about "bwbachod".'

To her credit, she did not dwell on thoughts of hobgoblins and soon forgot the episode in enjoying her bread and milk supper. Then went to her little room to fall into a dreamless sleep until daylight dawned.

The next evening, calling at an old friend's house with her aunt and sitting around the peat fire there with a few others who had dropped in to indulge, as was their wont, in a friendly chat, the subject cropped up again as they told how Jane had fancied there was a 'bwbach' and frightened the girls.

This started tale after tale of reminiscence, as first one and then another told of hair-raising experiences that had ultimately been fully explained away in simple manner, but which at the time had apparently been very terrifying.

Some of the facts as recounted by the tale-teller made Mary Eleanor's flesh creep, and her eyes open wide with wonder and credulity, because of the convincing manner in which the story was told.

Solemnly and slowly, and with true dramatic emphasis, some of the things that had happened in the long past of their lives, or their parents' or grandparents' lives, were gone over and worked up to in true Celtic manner.

'Yn wir, yn wir,' (indeed, indeed,) was an asseveration of frequent repetition in the exciting narratives, and Mary Eleanor had frequently to cast a glance at her aunt's face to catch a wink of reassurance and the slight smile that seemed to convey to her that these tales were some of the 'silly rubbish' spoken of the night before.

There were tales of how someone had heard noises and groans that had never been quite cleared up before someone's death, and how, one night, an 'ystlumen-nos' (bat) had kept flying around in someone else's bedroom, and that they had heard of a death in the family the very next day – the bat had come as an omen of ill, as it always did.

This ·was followed by one of the party asking if they had ever seen a 'canwyll gorff' (corpse candle).

'No, indeed to goodness, we should go mad if we did,' they declared.

'Well,' was the slow impressive reply, 'they tell me you can see one any night in the old cemetery at the next village. I have not seen it myself, but the Vicar says it is not what people say it is; he says it is some kind of gas that lights itself when it comes up from the earth to the air. I don't think I'd like to see it myself though. But the Vicar is a great scholar, and he ought to know.'

'Well,' replied one of the group, 'I've heard of a Jack-o-Lantern or two on the bog at night and some people are afraid to go in that direction after dark'.

'It *does* make one feel creepy to talk of all these things. I shall be afraid to go home tonight if we can't explain them,' said another.

'I don't think one need worry over a Jack-o-Lantern. The English call it Will-of-the-wisp more often than Jack-o-Lantern, don't they, Mary Eleanor?' queried her aunt, purposely bringing her into the conversation.

'Yes, I know what you all mean now,' she answered. 'Perhaps your lights are something like the little fireflies we used to catch in America. I have seen them dancing as thick as stars over the fields at night when I have been out.'

'Oh, my goodness! A field full of lights!' exclaimed a timid one. 'It would kill me!'

Laughing heartily, Mary Eleanor said she had caught some in her hands many a time, and they were only little innocent flies that would not hurt anybody, and the Jack-o-Lanterns she knew, she told them were made out of a big pumpkin hollowed out, and a few holes cut in it to represent eyes, nose, and mouth, and a candle put in it after dark.

Then somebody said it was very likely that some of the lights that simple people thought were ghostly were only little glow-worms or something that could be explained away in a similar manner.

'You can say what you like about lights,' put

in one who had hitherto been rather quiet. I know where there is a ghostly light that shows nearly every night and it is on the Common at the back of our house. It is not a bright light, and sometimes it is bigger than at other times. Old Mari and I went as close as we dared to it the other night but we could not make it out. I went there by day but all there is in that place is an old spar that is rotten that was put there last summer when they dragged it from the beach. It must be a ghost of some sort.'

Shaking with laughter at the credulous superstition evinced in the manner of the speaker, the one who had cleared up the mystery of the corpse candle said to her, 'If you and Mari put a rope around that spar and get someone to pull it away for you, your ghost will disappear. It is a very old spar and rotten in some places, and the light you see on it is phosphorescence. Just the same thing that you see on the herrings when they get damp when hung up outside if we have a spell of wet weather, or sometimes you can see it on the sea, you know, if you are looking out at night from the back fences.'

'But it is a big piece of light,' asserted the woman, unconvinced.

'There is a big patch of rotten wood on that spar. I know, for I was one of those who helped pull it up and it was good for nothing but firewood!' replied the man.

'Well, indeed, that's enough for one night of such talk. We'll leave the ysprydion (spirits) alone to settle the question between them, and all say "Goodnight",' said one, rising.

'Nos dawch,' and 'Noswaith dda i chi,' came mixed with laughter from the departing neighbours, with remarks that it was nice to have a full moon to show the way home that night, as they had all been rather worked up talking over such fear-inspiring things.

It was scarcely a week following that Mary Eleanor on coming home from school asked her elders what 'rheibio' meant.

'Some of the girls say that there is an old woman in the village who can do it. Who is she and where does she live?' she asked.

'My dear child, no one does such a thing now. By "rheibio" they mean that the old woman can cast a spell of sickness, or ill luck, or something like that, over persons or things she has a spite against them,' said her aunt.

'The girls say that old Shani does it, and that there are others, and they are all afraid of her a little because she does it. The other week she could not get butter at the farm, they say, and so she indulged in this thing they call "rheibio" – and they say she twiddles her fingers when she does it, and mumbles, and looks cross – and they have had trouble at the farm with the cows and the butter ever since and they say little Johnny Jones has been sick because his mother forgot an errand old Shani asked her to do and oh! there is a lot they say about her!' Mary Eleanor concluded.

'So it would seem by your long story. I don't think that is quite true. It may look like it but most of us know better than the very old people do, and don't believe it is in any human being's power to do such things,' was the reply she received.

'Well, Aunt,' she said, 'you know old Shani *does* look like an old witch.

'Have you ever seen an old witch?' asked her aunt.

'Well, no,' Mary Eleanor hesitantly replied. 'No, I haven't, but the pictures in books that tell us about fairies and witches make the witches seem to be very like old Shani. She has a funny thin face with a big hooked nose, and her hair is always hanging down over her forehead untidily and she has such piercing sharp little eyes, and she always has that ragged black shawl over her head so that you cannot see her very plainly. But I don't mind that so much as her hands. Ugh! I don't like to see them. She holds her shawl together tightly under her chin, and her hands look thin and her crooked-up fingers have got such awful nails, they look like claws! She has a very nasty temper too, the girls say. No wonder they say she is an old witch!' commented Mary Eleanor.

'I think the best way to think of her is as a poor old woman who has no one to care for her now, and who has grown neglectful of herself, and has also grown cross because of others' neglect, and because she feels slighted. One cannot really help one's looks, and I daresay if old Shani was kindly treated, she would respond by being a bit more pleasant. She certainly has a sharp tongue and temper, but we'll look on it in a charitable way and consider that past circumstances are in part at least responsible for her present appearance. I know she has had a hard life, poor thing,' said her aunt.

'I suppose she cannot help her looks, but she is so dirty in appearance, and those fingernails look awful. One cannot help shrinking away from her,' replied Mary Eleanor, 'even if one pities her.'

'It may be as well though to remember that because she is old, dirty, and neglected, she is not able to bewitch any body or any thing,' was her aunt's admonition. 'Don't listen to the girls' chatter about her. That things have happened badly for those who have had anything to do with her is merely coincidence.'

Mary Eleanor on thinking over her aunt's advice, and the schoolgirls' silly gossip came to the conclusion that it would be just as well not to credit all that was said about poor old Shani, and recalled the time when the bwbach scare had half frightened them coming home from the Band of Hope meeting, and it had proved to be nothing but the poor old donkey, after all.

Perhaps a similar simple solution to all that was said about old Shani's supernatural powers might sometime be found. In Mary Eleanor's opinion, poor old Shani would look better if she was not so cross and dirty and she thought someone ought to tell her that she had dirty ears, for being old, perhaps she could not see, and anyway there were only two very small windows in the tiny house where she lived so perhaps she was really not to blame for not seeing where she was dirty, and did not know that she had grown dirty and repulsive.

She came to the conclusion that she need not be afraid of her, however, and avoid her as some of the girls did. Perhaps if a chance occurred when she could do the poor old woman a kindness, it would help to take the cross look from her face.

Having thus satisfactorily settled to her own content the reputed abilities of poor old Shani in the line of witchcraft, Mary Eleanor dismissed her from her mind.

The next day in school, a group of her schoolmates were heard discussing the exploits of some of the older lads on the previous weekend when they had attempted entering the 'Twll y Ladi Wen', (White Ladies' [sic] Hole), a large hole in the near side of the cliffs.

Climbing up to it from the shingle below, some of the lads had lit candles and gone in quite a distance to explore it. It had not been very comfortable going in; they could not stand upright, as it was only about four feet high inside.

Mary Eleanor asked the girls why it was called the White Ladies' Hole, and one of them volunteered the statement that a lady dressed all in white was sometimes seem to emerge from the hole and wander about as if in distress.

Another girl said that her father said it was probably an old shaft where at one time someone had tried to find lead. A third said it led in a long distance under the cliffs and that it was a hole used by smugglers years and years ago.

Mary Eleanor's experiences of the recounting of ghostly and weird tales during the winter had been, happily for her, such that a simple solution for all uncanny things mentioned was found, and she put away from her mind the thought of a poor ghostly White Lady, and thought it was possibly one of the other solutions which would prove to be the origin of the White Ladies' Hole.

She had grown more self-reliant in respect of the girls' gossip, and while she joined in with them in fun and play and merry chatter, she reserved the right to think for herself and by skilful questioning and observation elicit all she could relating to any subject under discussion, such accumulations of information to be conned over in her quiet leisure hours, which were many.

Extremely fond of reading, Mary Eleanor had avidly read and reread *Smiles' Duty* until she almost knew it by heart, also a book about shipwrecked mariners that took her in fancy to the Isles of the Pacific and about which she wove many a fanciful tale of possible adventure when she grew up.

The very few other English books that came into her possession were hungrily read, and even a few dry old books of sermons were gone through, as well as an ancient Geography book which had old-fashioned type throughout and in which most of the s's were f's – anything to assuage the reading itch which intensified daily. She had to guess at the meaning of some of the big words, as there was no dictionary available excepting the old English–Welsh one, which, while finding her English translations for Welsh words, and vice-versa, did not explain any of the words.

In the reading books in her school some

definitions of the bigger words were met with at the end of each reading lesson, and Mary Eleanor seldom had to glance at these more than once as her memory was extremely retentive when it was a question of reading and finding out just what words meant.

Poetry was as welcome to her as prose, for it appealed to her sense of beauty and she could enjoy reading a book of poems as much as a storybook, for the music of the rhymes and the cadence of the phrases helped to satisfy her craving for the beautiful in all things.

With a mind thus ever open to search out for and receive impressions from all sources, with an intuitive selectiveness that came naturally to her, Mary Eleanor was able to absorb and retain whatever was beneficial to her in mind and body and separate the gold from the dross of life as day succeeded day in her little sphere.

She was nonetheless as much of a child as any girl of her age and joined heartily in all her schoolmates' games and fun and chatter, and was as quick as any of them to find cause for merriment in many a little episode of school life, though seldom indulging in fun and laughter directed toward a fellow schoolmate.

Sensitive to a degree herself, she could not bear to see anyone teased overmuch, and never called attention to any little happening which, while amusing to herself, might hurt the feelings of the boy or girl if advertised to the class.

She was frequently asked to help her school friends work out their arithmetic examples or tell them how to analyse the portion of prose or poetry allotted to them. Sensing the difficulties they met with in placing parts of speech under their correct heading by realising the stupidity and ignorance she would evince if asked to attempt the same thing in Welsh, she willingly assisted them whenever possible, although it ever remained to her a doubtful question as to whether she ought to tell her teacher that she did it for them.

A few tactful questions to the assisted ones by the teacher frequently elicited the fact that the work was not their unaided endeavour, and she would own up to helping them because they wanted it explained again, and would do better next time by themselves.

It was customary in the village for the majority of the girls to stay at school until they were thirteen or fourteen years of age, the last year or a portion thereof, according to the means of the parents, being spent in a local Ladies' School, to finish off and give a certain polish to the deportment and a fillip towards the attainment of grown-up young ladies' manners.

Mary Eleanor saw many an older girl leave for a quarter or two of finishing at the Young Ladies' School. A few of them stayed a couple of years and benefited thereby, but she did not think that those who went for a brief quarter could possibly absorb much of the many new subjects taken up because their proficiency in English varied with each girl. She had been amused at the story of one schoolgirl who had been sent to London to visit relatives as a finish to schooldays instead of taking the Ladies' School course.

On her return to the village, she said she had forgotten how to speak in her native tongue, as she had been so long in London, quite a 'blwyddyn ond three quarters' (year but three quarters) thus making a laughable mixture of English and Welsh.

Mary Eleanor was not at all eager to follow in their footsteps, for her present school was just across the road from her home, and it was a convenience when playtime came to run across the road and get a bite to eat, a fact which mattered very much to her just now as she seemed to be in a chronic state of hunger consequent on her rapid growth, and a titbit was always welcome to appease the appetite until time came for the appointed meals.

The complete change in her life tended to growth of body and mind, and character, as each season brought new delights of beach and bog, friends and fancies, and Mary Eleanor with her thirst for knowledge eagerly assimilated the greater portion of all that fell to her lot in school, at home or at play, much of which as she grew older she learned to discard if not likely to prove beneficial to her. Ambitious ever, she had realised that application was the only way to conquer a hard lesson and she learned to take a deal of patience with things worthwhile doing in order to accomplish in the best manner whatever she took in hand.

Acknowledgements

First of all, I would like to thank my paternal great-grandmother for writing such a thoughtful piece, and for all her other writings, especially her careful chronicling of my great-grandfather Captain Thomas Jones's voyages and exploits. In particular, though, I want to credit my parents for inspiring my fascination with my family's history. I have been aware of Captain Thomas Jones's achievements all my life, it seems, but only learned of Amey Jane's extraordinary life and writings at around the age of ten. I now live about fifteen minutes from Estyn Grange, Hope, where she wrote *Mary Eleanor*, and my son Dominic lives round the corner from the house, so I can see it regularly and dream about what went on in my great-grandmother's head as she was writing this manuscript there eighty years ago.

Thank you to my cousin Janet Greenwell, who is also Amey Jane's great-granddaughter, who has shared her family research with me, and to another cousin, Jean Verney, who made me realise that Mary Eleanor stands for 'me'! I am also grateful to a very distant cousin Kenneth Smallbone, who many years ago shared with me his research into the Hyde branch of John Lewis's antecedents, right back to the sixteenth century.

Andrew Nickson of Eclipse Studios deserves a special mention, for his beautiful cover art and for his knowledge of the self-publishing process once the editing process is complete, and to my children Patrick and Charlotte for proofreading and helping with layout. Novel editing is my business, but I never get involved in the actual process of book design and publication. I now have a new respect for my authors and all they still have to do when their manuscript leaves my hands!

Lastly, thank you to you, the reader, whether you are a relative, close or distant – perhaps a descendant of one of Amey's siblings living in the USA or Canada – a resident of Ceredigion, a visitor to a museum, a historian, or you've just picked up this book because you were intrigued by the cover. Perhaps you have just moved to a small town yourself – maybe somewhere in Wales. Without readers, books would literally not be worth the paper they are printed on.

Connect with me at lesley@mary-eleanor.co.uk. If you are interested in my editing services, visit my website perfecttheword.co.uk

Printed in Great Britain
by Amazon